West Point

THE FIRST 200 YEARS

West Point

THE FIRST 200 YEARS

The COMPANION to the PBS™ TELEVISION SPECIAL

Foreword by Buzz Aldrin

John Grant,
James M. Lynch, *and* Ronald H. Bailey

Ted Spiegel, Principal Photographer

The
Globe
Pequot
Press

Guilford, Connecticut

Jacket and text design by Casey Shain
Jacket back photos: (top) USMA Archives; (bottom left and right) © Ted Spiegel

Photo credits: pp. v, ix, xii, xvi, 10, 28, 62, 71 (top), 95 (painting), 96, 120, 134–35 (bottom), 152, 154 (bottom): © Ted Spiegel; pp. vi–xi (background),147, 176–83 (background), 178 (seal): USMA Archives; pp. xiii, 2 (drum), 7, 8 (pistol), 9, 20 (both), 24 (rifle), 26 (top), 31, 46 (bottom), 47 (top), 57, 59 (painting), 74 (drawing), 78, 88 (both), 90 (right), 91, 95 (top), 97, 101, 110 (top), 111 (letter), 117 (bottom), 126, 129 (robe), 134 (jersey), 145 (both), 147 (coat), 149 (bottom), 178 (fan), 179 (medal and memorabilia), 182 (portrait): Julie Bidwell; pp. 83, 104: © Bob Krist; p. 168 (bottom): © Robert Stewart. All other credits appear with the photographs.

Photographs by Robert Stewart reprinted with permission from *The Corps of Cadets: A Year at West Point* by Robert Stewart © 1996

Video captures courtesy Driftwood Productions

The "See It On PBS" logo and the PBS Mark are trademarks of the Public Broadcasting Service and are used with permission.

Library of Congress Cataloging-in-Publication Data
Grant, John, 1948-
    West Point: the first 200 years: the companion to the PBS television special / by John Grant,
James M. Lynch, and Ronald H. Bailey.
        p. cm.
    Includes bibliographical references and index.
    ISBN 0-7627-1013-6
    1. United States Military Academy—History. I. Lynch, James M., 1952- II. Bailey, Ronald H.
III. Title.
U410.L1 G73 2002
355'.0071'173—dc21   2001040820

Printed in Canada
First Edition/First Printing

This book is dedicated to the nearly sixty thousand men and women who have graduated from the United States Military Academy and have gone on to serve their country at home and abroad.

Contents

I was only seventeen when I first reported to West Point on July 1, 1947, and although I had come from a military tradition—my father had served in the Army Air Corps and my mother was the daughter of an Army chaplain—I was not quite ready for what greeted me. As soon as we arrived, upperclassmen ordered all of us new cadets to roll up the legs of our civilian trousers precisely five inches, supposedly so we could see whether our feet were properly pointed. It also served to remind us that first-year cadets—plebes—were too dumb to figure this out without actually looking.

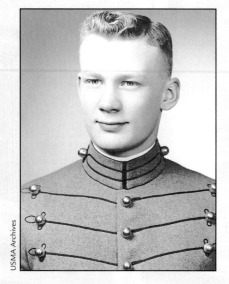

USMA Archives

This was the beginning of the West Point process of making us followers so we could be leaders. In the classroom we had to be ready to snap to attention and recite a lesson at a moment's notice. In athletics we learned physical conditioning, teamwork, and the esprit de corps that made us feel proud to be part of a larger organization. And during practically every waking moment, we cadets endured the kind of regimentation that creates the discipline necessary for leadership.

The values instilled at West Point stood all of us in good stead for our future careers. Upon graduation I was commissioned in the Air Force and went on to serve my country in a way I had dreamed of as a boy—flying jet fighters. I flew on sixty-six combat missions during the Korean War. Later, the engineering-oriented curriculum I had experienced at West Point helped prepare me for doctoral studies in manned space rendezvous at MIT. The principles of discipline and teamwork that I learned at the

Academy proved invaluable after I was selected as an astronaut for the Gemini and Apollo space programs, which culminated in 1969 when Neil Armstrong and I walked on the moon.

Much has changed at West Point in the half century since I graduated. The Corps of Cadets more accurately reflects American society by including women, African Americans, and others largely excluded in earlier days. The rigid curriculum has been loosened up to allow cadets freedom to select a major and choose electives that will better prepare them for a constantly changing world. What remains the same, however, after two hundred years is West Point's mission to mold young citizen-patriots into members of the Long Gray Line—men and women of character who will help lead us in confronting the challenges of this new millennium.

BUZZ ALDRIN

NOVEMBER 2001

Colonel Buzz Aldrin, USMA Class of 1951 (USAF, retired), became the second man to walk on the moon and is a leading advocate of expanded space exploration.

ACKNOWLEDGMENTS

West Point: The First 200 Years and *West Point*, the companion PBS documentary, would not have been possible without the cooperation of the U.S. Military Academy (USMA) at West Point. We are grateful to the current superintendent, Lieutenant General William J. Lennox Jr., and his predecessor, Lieutenant General Daniel W. Christman.

The Public Affairs Office at West Point was essential to the successful completion of our work. We are particularly grateful for the tireless efforts of Lieutenant Colonel James E. Whaley III, director of public affairs for the USMA. From our first meeting to our seemingly endless requests for assistance, Jim was always cooperative, friendly, and helpful. Andrea Hamburger and Michael D'Aquino, public affairs specialists, also provided valuable assistance.

Dr. Stephen B. Grove, historian at the U.S. Military Academy, was an invaluable contributor to this book. Not only did Steve review the manuscript for accuracy, he provided important guidance to the authors, as well as the television producer, throughout the development of the book and TV program.

We are indebted to the staff at the USMA Library, most especially Suzanne Christoff, associate director for special collections and archives, and Alicia Mauldin, archives technician. Our sincere thanks also go out to the staff at the West Point Museum, including director Michael Moss and curators David Reel, Michael McAfee, and Robert Fisch.

Funding for the television documentary was provided by the Public Broadcasting

Service (PBS). We are thankful for the support and confidence of PBS co-chief program executive John Wilson and senior director of factual programming Sandy Heberer.

Oregon Public Broadcasting (OPB) was our coproduction partner for the television documentary, and we are grateful to President and CEO Maynard Orme and Senior Vice President John Lindsay for the ongoing relationship with OPB. John Booth and Cheri Arbini of OPB provided tireless assistance in support of the television program. Jack McDonald, the television producer-writer, made valuable contributions to the book.

I am grateful for having had the opportunity to work with Jim Lynch and Ron Bailey. Both are superb history writers who were able to grasp the subject matter and present it in a clear and comprehensible style. I am especially thankful to Ron for his willingness to provide assistance at a critical time in the writing process.

West Point: The First 200 Years represents the fourth book I have done with the Globe Pequot Press. I am grateful for this relationship and especially for the support provided for this book by executive editor Laura Strom and associate editor Himeka Curiel.

The great pleasure in developing projects like *West Point: The First 200 Years* is being able to share them with my family. My wife, Joan, and son, Andy, are a constant source of pride and encouragement.

JOHN GRANT
DRIFTWOOD PRODUCTIONS

INTRODUCTION

From its headwaters in the Adirondack Mountains, the Hudson River flows due south with hardly a twist or turn for more than two hundred miles through a beautiful valley of green pastures and forest-clad granite hills. Then, after slipping through a narrow gap between two particularly lofty, broad-shouldered peaks called Storm King and Breakneck Ridge, the stream collides head-on with a flat-topped promontory towering almost two hundred feet above the waterline. Over the ages this stratum of harder rock has resisted the current's erosive power, forcing it into an abrupt, right-angle bend to the east. Scarcely a quarter mile farther on, the Hudson, having flanked this indomitable barrier, makes another ninety-degree turn and resumes a southward course for some fifty-odd miles to the sea.

Seth Eastman's View of West Point (circa 1840) shows the Military Academy campus in the spectacular setting of the Hudson River Valley. A cadet, instructor, and Civil War veteran, Eastman was one of the few West Pointers to become known as a painter.

The point of land jutting into the river from the west bank is noteworthy not only for its unusual topography and the sublime vistas stretching out in every direction, but also for the great drama of human events that has played out on the broad, grassy plain crowning its summit. West Point—the name reverberates through the annals of American history from its earliest pages right down to the present day. The site would play a pivotal role in General George Washington's defensive strategy during the Revolutionary War—and also serve as the catalyst for another American general's indelible act of treachery. West Point's most enduring fame, however, stems from the military academy established there by the founding fathers of a fledgling democratic nation. "It could not stand on more appropriate ground," Charles Dickens remarked during a visit, "and any ground more beautiful can hardly be."

Leaders of American land forces in most major battles from the Civil War to Desert Storm learned their trade at this school. Other graduates' greatest contributions were in a civilian capacity; they built railroads and canals, providing the infrastructure necessary for America's expansion, or they surveyed the rugged, unknown territories of the West during the nation's infancy. Additionally, many of these career soldiers would serve their country later in life as politicians, statesmen, or diplomats. Two would ultimately become president of the United States; two others would walk on the moon.

Over the last two hundred years, the cadets attending the United States Military Academy have come from every corner of America, every political persuasion, every economic circumstance, and—more recently—every ethnic background and both genders as well. But no matter how disparate their personal histories before arriving at this hallowed venue on the banks of the Hudson, they subsequently shared a common bond, the depth of which is not easily understood by those who have not lived in its barracks and drilled on its Plain; they all spent their defining years at West Point, truly a place of legendary figures and legendary deeds.

The United States Military Academy, founded on March 16, 1802, is located approximately 50 miles north of New York City in the picturesque Hudson River Valley.
© Bob Krist

CHAPTER ONE

1609—1782

A Place
of Legends

In 1609, when Henry Hudson first sailed up the river that would bear his name—negotiating the tight, difficult S-turn at West Point en route—he found a rich land, well watered and brimming with virgin hardwood forests. He also discovered an indigenous population that was amenable to bartering with Europeans. "The natives are a very good people," Hudson recorded, noting that "they supposed I was afraid of their bows, and taking the arrows they broke them in pieces and threw them into the fire." The lucrative trade that developed in the wake of Hudson's visit convinced his Dutch sponsors that colonization was a desirable next step.

In 1624 the first immigrants from the Netherlands arrived with a mandate to "advance the peopling of fruitful and unsettled parts." These earliest white settlers, who established farms in the wild glens and settlements along the riverbank, not only bequeathed many of the Hudson Valley's lyrical place-names but also gave a Dutch flavor to the region that lingers to this day.

England's victory in 1664 over the Netherlands for control of its New World colonies changed the valley's political masters, as well as some labels—New Amsterdam, for example, became New York—but did not displace the Dutch inhabitants; it merely added a wave of English settlers to the mix. As generations passed, however, the people no longer thought of themselves as either Dutch or English—though they retained their

This undated colored engraving, Henry Hudson Greeted by Native Americans, *depicts an encounter between the Dutch explorer and the indigenous people of the area now known as the Hudson River Valley.*

© Bettmann/CORBIS

King George III ruled over the colonies with a heavy hand.

This ornate eighteenth-century British military kettle drum was captured by American forces at the Battle of Saratoga. It is part of the collection of the West Point Museum, the oldest and largest military museum in the country.

loyalty to the Crown—but rather as New Yorkers and, in a larger sense, Americans.

During colonial times the Hudson River became a vital artery of trade and transportation leading from the burgeoning port of New York City into the continent's emergent hinterlands. Towns along its banks as far north as Albany thrived. But West Point, with high bluffs dropping precipitously to the river's edge, proved unsuitable for commercial docks. Furthermore, the sharp turns in the Hudson that define the site, coupled with tricky currents and gusting winds that often whistle through the steep valley, made it difficult for sailing ships to land there. The promontory languished as an anonymous parcel of a landholder's large estate. But that obscurity was about to change dramatically, for all the factors that rendered West Point disadvantageous to commerce and settlement would prove a strategic godsend when fighting broke out between the American colonies and the English Crown in 1775.

The Revolutionary War began in New England where disaffection with King George III and Parliament's capricious, heavy-handed rule ran highest. The British, whose overwhelming naval power gave them control of the seas, sought to blockade New England's coastline and then isolate the region from the rest of the colonies with an overland assault. The strategy made perfect sense and was no secret to their American opponents, who could just as easily deduce the logical avenue of attack. New York's Provincial Congress counseled: "If the enemy persist in their plan of subjugating these States to the yoke of Great Britain, they must . . . be more and more convinced of the necessity of their becoming masters of the Hudson River, which will . . . effectually prevent all intercourse between the eastern and southern [states], divide our strength, and enfeeble every effort for our common preservation and security." General George Washington—named commander in chief of American forces by the Continental Congress—agreed, and harbored no doubts as to what constituted the lynchpin of the entire Hudson Valley position. West Point, he later declared, was "the most important military position in America."

In August 1776, when British forces drove Washington's largely untried Continental Army out of New York City, the threat to the Hudson became bona fide and immediate. The Americans had already begun to fortify the West Point area. Unfortunately, the engineer in charge chose to ignore the natural advantages of the west bank and instead built field fortifications and placed his artillery batteries on the lower ground of Constitution Island, directly across the river from West Point.

His mistake became apparent in the fall of 1777 as the British launched a three-pronged offensive: One column headed south from Canada through the Lake Champlain region toward the upper Hudson Valley, while another, smaller force pressed eastward from Lake Ontario. A third column under General Sir Henry Clinton later advanced up the Hudson from New York City with the aim of joining the other two at Albany. The American positions on Constitution Island fell to Clinton without a fight, and he continued moving upriver to the state capital at Kingston unopposed. The American cause teetered on the verge of disaster, but at this crucial juncture Clinton received news that the British column from the west had turned back and the entire force descending from Canada had been captured near Saratoga. Unable to secure his gains without reinforcement, Clinton razed the fieldworks on Constitution Island and withdrew to New York City. The area reverted to American hands.

This portrait by John Gadsby Chapman shows George Washington as a colonel of the Virginia militia in 1772.

To avoid a repetition of this near catastrophe, plans were immediately initiated to build proper fortifications on the high ground along the west bank. That winter a brigade of Continental troops arrived to garrison the area and undertake the construction. The Hudson was frozen over, and one of the foot soldiers recorded for posterity—albeit with atrocious spelling—that on January 27, 1778, the troops "marched over the Rever on the ise [and] marched back again for thar was no Place to Loge theor on the West side of the Rever." A handful of his comrades did, however, remain on the far shore that night, marking an important milestone in the history of West Point: Beginning with that frigid winter day in a distant, long-ago war, American troops have occupied the site with nary a single interruption, making West Point the oldest continuously garrisoned U.S. Army post in the world.

> **IF THE ENEMY PERSIST IN THEIR PLAN OF SUBJUGATING THESE STATES TO THE YOKE OF GREAT BRITAIN, THEY MUST ... BE MORE AND MORE CONVINCED OF THE NECESSITY OF THEIR BECOMING MASTERS OF THE HUDSON RIVER."**
>
> — NEW YORK'S PROVINCIAL CONGRESS

With the spring thaw, work on the fortifications began in earnest. This coincided with the arrival of Colonel Thaddeus Kosciuszko, a Polish officer who had volunteered his

PLAN
OF
WEST POINT.

Copied from the Original Map of
Major VILLEFRANCHE (Engineer)

Scale of a Mile

Villefranche Eng.

THE GREAT CHAIN

This map originally drawn by Major de Villefranche, chief engineer at West Point after Kosciuszko, shows the positioning of the Great Chain across the Hudson.

USMA Archives

Alarmed by British general Sir Henry Clinton's successful advance up the Hudson Valley in the fall of 1777, George Washington ordered the commander of Continental troops in that area to "employ your whole force and all the means in your power for erecting and completing . . . such works and obstructions as may be necessary to defend and secure the river against any future attempts of the enemy." In addition to the batteries and earthen fortifications hurriedly constructed at West Point, the defenders decided that the river itself should be blocked to prevent British ships from passing upstream.

A quartermaster officer on Washington's staff contracted with the owner of the nearby Sterling Iron Works to forge a great chain with links two feet long and two and a quarter inches thick. The chain was constructed at the foundry in ten-link segments weighing half a ton each. The individual sections were transported by oxcart to the riverbank and floated downriver to West Point where they were joined together into a continuous length measuring some five hundred yards. Then the chain was attached to fifteen log rafts that were coated with pitch to keep the wood from becoming waterlogged.

On April 30, 1778, the chain was floated into the river and secured to capstans on each shore. Until war's end, the chain would be hauled in every winter before ice choked the river, and then repositioned in spring. The British chose not to challenge the strong defenses at West Point, so the chain's effectiveness against wooden-hulled ships was never tested. Thirteen of its massive iron rings can be seen today at Trophy Point on the grounds of the Military Academy, a tangible "link" to West Point's long and storied history.

services to the American side. Trained in the science of military engineering, Kosciuszko provided an invaluable contribution to West Point's defense. With a practiced eye, he positioned four artillery batteries along the bank in just the right positions to engage enemy ships as they slowed to maneuver through the river's tight bends.

Surely the most innovative aspect of West Point's defense was a huge iron chain that was strung from the west bank to Constitution Island in the middle of the Hudson's challenging S-curve, where approaching ships would already have lost much of their headway. To protect the fortress—and to guard against attack from the landward side—an earthen citadel with walls as much as twenty feet thick and thirteen feet high was raised on

Trophy Point offers what is considered the most famous view on the Hudson River. This British Howitzer was captured at the Battle of Saratoga. Also pictured is a section of the Great Chain—one clevis, one swivel and thirteen links—that was placed at Trophy Point prior to the Civil War.

© Ted Spiegel

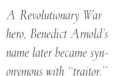

the northeast corner of the grassy plain at the edge of the steep cliffs. This facility was named Fort Arnold in honor of Benedict Arnold, a militia officer from Connecticut who had risen through the ranks to become a major general. Arnold had demonstrated inspired leadership and personal courage on the battlefield during the American victories at Fort Ticonderoga and Saratoga, as well as the unsuccessful invasion of Canada. In these early days of the war, he had distinguished himself as one of the Continental Army's rising stars.

Polish officer Thaddeus Kosciuszko, one of many foreigners who aided Americans during the Revolutionary War, was given responsibility for planning the defense and fortifications at West Point in 1778.

National Archives

Meanwhile, West Point's defenders settled into the routine of garrison life. On the Plain they learned the intricacies of close-order drill under the barked commands of Baron Friedrich von Steuben, an experienced Prussian officer who, like Kosciuszko, had rallied to the upstart nation's cause. It is also quite possible that engineers and artillerists assigned to the post received instruction in their specialized fields, although no formal school was established at West Point during the war. For recreation, there were occasional balls and soirees to which local inhabitants received invitations. One soldier pronounced: "The Dutch Girls are generally pretty well looking and entertaining, but have large ankles."

On the military front British general Sir Henry Clinton launched one final venture up the Hudson in spring of 1779. After some initial success, lack of reinforcements and a devastating night assault led by "Mad" Anthony Wayne at the British position at Stony Point again forced him to retreat before he even reached Kosciuszko's bastion at West Point. Clinton then decided on a change of strategy: He turned his attention south, hoping to catch and crush the Continental Army in one decisive victory and end the rebellion. From that point on, Fort Arnold would face its gravest threat not from the British but from its own namesake.

A Revolutionary War hero, Benedict Arnold's name later became synonymous with "traitor."

National Archives

Owing to the impressive record he had compiled in the war's initial campaigns, Benedict Arnold was named commander of the Philadelphia military district in 1778. But his fortunes suffered a dramatic down-turn; the profligate lifestyle he and his wife pursued amid the city's high society had left the general deeply in debt. Moreover, Pennsylvania authorities had accused him of violating regulations in the discharge of his duties—though a court-martial cleared him of wrongdoing. He also felt slighted by the promotion of certain officers with less seniority over him.

The weight of these factors combined to persuade the once ardent patriot to sell out his own side. In the winter of 1779 he sent a secret message to Sir Henry Clinton, offering his services to the British in return for money. Clinton assigned his aide, Major John André, to handle the details. Over the following months André and the disenchanted American general covertly corresponded on a regular basis. Arnold, meanwhile, had decided on the prize that would elicit the greatest reward from his British patrons. He connived to have himself transferred to West Point—not too difficult to arrange for a war hero of his stature—and was

named commandant of the post in August 1780. He and André quickly concluded a deal: Arnold would hand over the fortifications, all of its ordnance, and the garrison in return for a commission in the British army and the "sum even of 20,000 pounds."

To Arnold's troops, their new commandant appeared the perfect picture of energy and enthusiasm as he went about his duties. But all the while Arnold

West Point Museum Collections, USMA

was surreptitiously conspiring to weaken West Point's defenses. He allocated his limited manpower to nonessential tasks rather than vital repairs on the field fortifications, and he cleverly reduced the pool of soldiers available for construction by increasing the number assigned to guard and sentry duty.

Finally, on September 21, the plan was set in motion. Arnold and André rendezvoused that night at an isolated spot on the Hudson between the opposing armies, where the American handed over documents detailing the post's defenses. Their meeting ran long, making it impossible for André to return under cover of darkness. He changed out of his uniform and into civilian clothes, hid the papers in his boot, and, armed with a pass signed by Arnold, set out on horseback for British lines.

En route he was stopped by three suspicious American militiamen. André produced the pass, but the soldiers insisted on searching this lone rider and quickly discovered the incriminating evidence. Their commanding officer, not yet suspecting Arnold's complicity, immediately sent word to West Point and forwarded the stolen documents to Washington's headquarters. This warning allowed Arnold to escape downriver on his personal barge to a waiting British ship. (André was not so lucky; he would be tried and eventually hung as a spy.)

Washington and his staff arrived at West Point for a previously scheduled visit. There the full scope of the plot was finally revealed. The post was clearly in a state of disarray,

Treason of Arnold by Charles F. Blauvelt (1857) shows U.S. General Benedict Arnold instructing British Major John André to conceal the plans for West Point in his boot. André was later captured by American militiamen, foiling Arnold's treasonous plot.

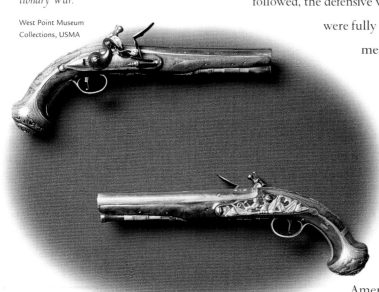

These flintlock officer's pistols are believed to have belonged to George Washington during the Revolutionary War.

West Point Museum Collections, USMA

Few regions in the country offer a greater combination of natural beauty and history than the dramatic landscapes that surround the U.S. Military Academy at West Point.

© Ted Spiegel

totally unprepared for a British attack. "Arnold had made such dispositions with the garrison," Alexander Hamilton noted, "as may tempt the enemy in its present weakness to make the stroke this night." Washington assumed personal command and immediately placed the troops on alert against an assault that, thankfully, never came. In the days that followed, the defensive works that Arnold had deliberately neglected were fully stocked and manned. Fort Arnold, meanwhile, was quickly renamed Fort Clinton, not for Sir Henry but in honor of James Clinton, who supervised the original construction of the fort.

If not for Major André's chance encounter with three wary militiamen, West Point could easily have fallen, changing the course—and perhaps even the outcome—of the war. Benedict Arnold, whose name became an American epithet for treason, went on to serve as a brigadier general in the British army. He subsequently conducted raids against his home state of Connecticut, burning more than 150 buildings. His troops massacred American militia at Fort Griswold, near New London, further staining his already infamous reputation.

In 1782 Arnold and his family sailed to England, where he acted as an adviser to the government on the conduct of the war. Yet he never gained complete acceptance from his benefactors; at war's end he was shunted aside as a distasteful reminder of a long and ultimately futile conflict. For his attempted betrayal of West Point, Arnold in the end received less than a third of the money he had been promised. Unable to return to America and scorned in his adopted homeland, the once exalted general died in London, broken and friendless, in June of 1801.

" THE PLEASANT AND HEALTHY SITUATION OF [WEST POINT] IS REMARKABLE FOR THE SALUBRITY OF ITS AIR. "

— GEORGE WASHINGTON

West Point enjoyed a more propitious fate. The campaigns that would decide the American Revolution were played out far to the south in Virginia and the Carolinas. Washington, however, ensured that West Point maintained a full garrison. On his orders, soldiers convalescing from wounds were sent to the post where, the commander in chief hoped, they would profit from "the pleasant and healthy situation of [West Point] which is remarkable for the salubrity of its air." Following his decisive triumph at Yorktown, which secured the colonies' independence, Washington returned to the Hudson and set up headquarters at the town of Newburgh just north of West Point.

In 1782 a colossal victory celebration took place on the grassy Plain next to Fort Clinton. Thirteen cannons fired multiple salutes, and Washington himself took the floor that evening as a military band played dance music in a seventeen-thousand-square-foot pavilion built especially for the occasion. It was a celebration of Louis Joseph, the heir apparent to the French throne. It was also an expression of thanks to the French for their critical support. The mood was self-congratulatory—and rightly so, for Washington's Continental Army, a creation of thirteen scattered colonies with meager resources for making war, composed of amateur citizen-soldiers often commanded by inexperienced, untrained officers, had just defeated the world's greatest military power. In the joy of the moment, the celebrants can be excused if they did not pause to consider what form of government would emerge from the crucible of revolution or what role the army— and the vital bastion of West Point— would play in the new nation's defense.

Revolutionary War powder horn made by Jasper March while he served at West Point (circa 1779).

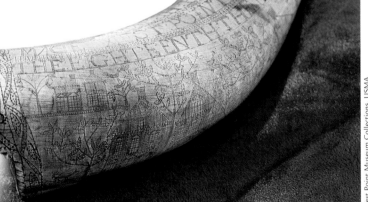

West Point Museum Collections, USMA

CHAPTER TWO

1782—1817

A TURBULENT BEGINNING

As far back as 1776, General Henry Knox,

Washington's chief of artillery in the Continental Army, had campaigned for the establishment of a national military academy. "And as officers can never act with confidence until they are masters of their profession," the visionary general told a congressional committee, "an Academy established on a liberal plan would be of the utmost service." He foresaw a school "where the whole theory and practice of fortification and gunnery should be taught." John Adams echoed that call, stating "we must make our young geniuses perfect masters of the Art of War in every branch." And at war's end, George Washington insisted on "the necessity of the proposed Institution, unless we intend to let the science [of war] become extinct, and to depend entirely upon the Foreigners for their friendly aid."

National Archives

Ironically, the ink had hardly dried on the 1783 Treaty of Paris, which guaranteed American sovereignty, before the founders of the new nation began systematically dismantling the military force that had secured their independence. State militia regiments went home, and their volunteer soldiers mustered out; the regular army, small to begin with, was drastically reduced. By 1784 the U.S. Army consisted of eighty men: twenty-five at the frontier outpost of Fort Pitt and fifty-five at West Point. The wartime talk of a permanent training school for officers was forgotten in the elation of victory and the rush toward disarmament.

"The Republic," observed Knox, "seems adverse to the permanency of an Army." Congress confirmed his view, proclaiming that "standing armies in time of

General Henry Knox, chief of artillery during the Revolutionary War, was an early advocate of a national military academy.

peace are inconsistent with the principles of republican government, dangerous to the liberties of a free people, and generally converted into destructive engines for establishing despotism." Indeed, there was widespread and deep-seated opposition among the country's leaders to any sizable, professional military establishment. Well versed in the classics, they were aware of how fledgling democracies dating back to ancient Greece had been subverted by military tyrants. And all knew the fate of the Roman Republic at the hands of an ambitious general named Julius Caesar, who commanded legions of troops personally loyal to him. The architects of the American Republic vowed that it would not happen here.

Washington himself took the lead by symbolically demonstrating that he was no Caesar: Three months after the peace treaty was signed, the general in chief resigned his commission and returned to Mount Vernon to pursue the quiet life of a gentleman farmer. He was replaced by Knox, who, given command of a mere skeleton force, retired in less than a year, leaving a brevet major as the senior ranking officer in the U.S. Army.

During the immediate postwar period, the country struggled through several years of ineffectual management— the new federal government had no authority to raise revenue and was altogether beholden to the will of the individual states—until the Constitution was ratified in 1789. This represented a

After commanding American troops to victory, General George Washington resigned his military commission and returned to life as a farmer in Mount Vernon, Virginia. Washington wanted to ease any apprehension that the victorious military might try to rule the new nation.

victory for the Federalist Party, whose adherents—including Knox, Alexander Hamilton, and George Washington—favored a strong central government. Congress quickly authorized an expansion of the regular army from its nadir of eighty troops to a strength of seven hundred, and then in April 1790, as tensions rose along the frontier, to slightly more than twelve hundred men. Still, no large permanent body of professional soldiers was envisioned or endorsed; additional manpower would be levied as needed from individual states.

Thus did America's first national defense policy emerge: A small regular army would garrison forts along the East Coast, the frontier, and at West Point, while militia units, formed at the state and local level, would provide the backbone of the country's military power. In the spirit of the already legendary "minuteman," the militia would be called to service in times of war or national emergency, then return to civilian life when the crisis had passed.

Yet no one could ignore the need for trained officers to lead these troops. And no one could forget the Continental Army's forced reliance on foreign officers such as Kosciuszko and von Steuben during the Revolution. That dependence had not changed in the years since: It was a sad but inescapable truth that very few American-born officers possessed the engineering skills necessary to design and build a fort—and only a handful had the knowledge required to properly sight the fort's guns. Furthermore, in clashes with Native Americans along the frontier, militia units led by untrained, part-time officers had suffered humiliating defeats, while regular troops with professional soldiers in charge had fared much better. Obviously, something had to be done.

West Point is the oldest continuously occupied military post in America. At sites like this one above Fort Putnam on West Point's west flank, visitors can see remnants of the fortifications built during the Revolutionary War.

© Ted Spiegel

When George Washington reluctantly emerged from retirement to become the nation's first president in 1789, he renewed his earlier call for the establishment of a military academy. In a message to Congress, he argued that "the improvement of the system of military defense ought to afford an opportunity for the study of those branches of the

[military] art which can scarcely ever be obtained by practice alone." But the president's sentiments were not universally shared.

On the emerging American political landscape, there was a faction—known as Republicans and led by Washington's own secretary of state, Thomas Jefferson—that feared the concentration of too much power in the hands of the federal government. He and his supporters believed that a military academy would serve as a breeding ground for elitist professional officers who could potentially undermine civilian authority. Jefferson framed his objection on legal grounds, asserting that "none of the specified powers given by the Constitution would authorize" such a school.

Without an act of Congress, a formal military academy could not be established; and although the legislature debated the issue, no action was taken. The executive branch, however, did what it could through the War Department to institute a training curriculum for officers. The program, as might be expected, was based at West Point.

Surprisingly, given its crucial role in the Revolution and its permanent army garrison, the property still remained under private ownership. The titleholder had repeatedly—and fruitlessly—petitioned the government for back rent and damages incurred during years of occupation. Finally, in 1790, Congress acted on an earnest request from General Knox, now the secretary of war, to buy the land. West Point, located at that "peculiar bend or turn of [the Hudson]" was, Knox stressed, "of the most decisive importance to the [river's] defense." As such, it was critical to the country's defense. For the sum of $11,085, the United States took possession of Fort Clinton, the Plain, and the surrounding acreage.

Little had been done since the war to maintain the fortifications; Congress simply had not provided the necessary funds. Several buildings survived in various states of disrepair. Much of the grassy Plain was overgrown with low scrub pine. The great chain and many cannon captured from the British were stored in warehouses near the river. In these lean years the venerable bastion's appearance was as inauspicious as the initial efforts to create an educational program for American officers.

Following the Revolutionary War, Secretary of State Timothy Pickering proposed the creation of a military academy at West Point where students might be trained as officers to command the defenses of the nation.

The first attempt to develop a training regimen began in 1794, when the Corps of Artillerists and Engineers was established with a mandate to school officers in both these specialized branches. At the same time, Congress created the rank of cadet to signify officer trainees attached to the Corps. Knox's successor, Timothy Pickering, took a special interest in the project, hoping that it might in time eliminate America's reliance on outside expertise. Also, the course of study might eventually be expanded into something more wide ranging, in which case, "its principal station [West Point]," Pickering noted somewhat prophetically, "may then become a school for the purpose mentioned."

In January 1796 Pickering appointed the French-born Revolutionary War veteran Stephen Rochefontaine to command the Corps and oversee the training classes at West Point. Unfortunately, Lieutenant Colonel Rochefontaine's insistence on strict discipline and forced attendance of instructional sessions quickly met with stiff resistance from the American officers in his charge. Within a month they had filed a formal grievance with the War Department, petulantly complaining that the commandant's actions served to "render the duty hard and disagreeable." In April the building in which classes were held burned down—some reports claimed that the officers themselves had set the fire—forcing Rochefontaine to switch his emphasis: "The want of a proper place to meet with the gentlemen upon theoretical instruction Since the Destruction of the officer Barrack has led me to Exercise oftener in the Field upon Manoeuvers of Field pieces and Infantry."

Relations between the French professional soldier and his American protégés continued to deteriorate. Not long after the fire, a young lieutenant cursed Rochefontaine to his face; the colonel in return struck him a blow with his sword hilt, and the two soon found themselves enmeshed in a duel. Fortunately, neither party suffered injury, but Rochefontaine was dismissed from his post in 1798, his training program viewed as a dismal failure.

Meanwhile, the country's need for officers had never been more urgent at any point since the end of the Revolution. Europe was embroiled in a general war, and tensions were

Fort Putnam was a key fortification in West Point's defenses during the Revolutionary War.

running high with America's former ally France. The threat of hostilities was real and imminent. President John Adams, Washington's successor, promptly tried to resurrect the program at West Point. Congress authorized the hiring of four instructors, but Adams could find only one qualified candidate. Adams named mathematics professor, George Baron, to run the program. He also selected twelve cadets to report to Baron for

Thomas Jefferson was an early opponent of a national military academy. As a member of George Washington's cabinet, Jefferson argued that creation of a military academy was unconstitutional. Later, as president, Jefferson signed the act that officially authorized establishment of the military school at West Point.

instruction. It was a small but significant step toward establishing a permanent institution, but with Adams's defeat in the election of 1800, the rest would have to wait for his successor.

Thomas Jefferson, the nation's third president, took office in 1801. The great statesman, author, scientist, and staunch Republican had undergone a remarkable change of heart on the subject of a national military academy since his days in Washington's cabinet. Whereas before he had voiced strenuous opposition, now, as president, Jefferson pushed the project with speed and energy.

Although he was a prolific writer, Jefferson left no precise explanation as to why he reversed himself, and the reasons are probably as multifaceted as the man. While not a soldier himself, Jefferson clearly saw the country's present and future need for officers proficient in the military sciences, even if the immediate danger of war with France had passed.

Beyond wartime exigencies, Jefferson may have seized the opportunity to create a school that would break with existing universities, which emphasized Greek, Latin, and religious studies. His academy, drawing students from throughout the country and focusing on the physical sciences and engineering, might become a sort of national university whose graduates could put their knowledge to use in a civilian as well as military capacity.

But Jefferson was also a politician, and he undoubtedly understood that a military academy under Republican auspices could provide benefits beyond simply turning out a cadre of trained soldiers and engineers. It was also an excellent opportunity to balance the army's officer corps of upperclass Federalists with a new crop of military leaders in the Republican mold. The recent example of the French Revolution—inspired by America's own—which fell prey to elitist elements, terror, and finally the autocracy of Napoleon, was fresh in Jefferson's mind.

The only qualified candidate Jefferson could find to take charge of the nascent program was a foreign officer. Major Louis de Tousard—another Revolutionary War veteran, who had learned his trade at the French military academy in Strasbourg—was ordered to "give all the assistance in your power in the instruction of such officers and

cadets as may be at West Point." He arrived in September 1801; that same month, classes got under way with a mathematics course taught by George Baron. Thus began an educational tradition at West Point that continues to this day. In a sense, this marked the actual inception of the long-sought military academy, though it still lacked congressional sanction to make it official.

Cadets today study a core curriculum that balances physical sciences and engineering with humanities and social sciences.

Insubordination—the same problem that had plagued Rochefontaine—cropped up again during this period. "All order and regulation," wrote one cadet, "either moral or religious, gave way to idleness, dissipation and irreligion." Baron became embroiled in a particularly ugly dispute with one of the cadets, Joseph Swift, over an order he sent the young officer via his personal attendant. When Swift refused to accept "a verbal order by any servant," the two argued heatedly. Baron labeled him "a mutinous young rascal," and Swift angrily leaped at his instructor. Baron made a dash for his quarters, bolted the door just ahead of his pursuer, and ran to an upstairs window, whereupon the two exchanged "coarse epithets."

"ALL ORDER AND REGULATION, EITHER MORAL OR RELIGIOUS, GAVE WAY TO IDLENESS, DISSIPATION AND IRRELIGION."

—WEST POINT CADET

In his own defense during the inquiry that followed, Swift wrote: "The officers of the post deemed Mr. Baron's conduct to be so ungentlemanly and irritating, that an apology could not be made to him." The War Department reprimanded the cadet but allowed him to stay at West Point. Baron, on the other hand, was court-martialed and dismissed.

Jefferson, meanwhile, had finally found an American-born officer with the qualifications to take the reins. Major Jonathan Williams, a grandnephew of Benjamin Franklin, was a brilliant scientist in his own right, having published a treatise with the daunting title *Thermometrical Navigation*. Here, the president hoped, was the man to usher in a new era and give the cadets a sense of purpose. "I have been indefatigable," Williams pledged, "in brushing up all my former mathematical knowledge and adding to the stock." He arrived at West Point at the end of 1801 and quickly recommended to Jefferson that the Corps of Artillerists and Engineers be split into its two equally specialized components.

Three months later, at President Jefferson's urging, the Republican-controlled Congress passed the Military Peace Establishment Act, creating a separate Corps of Engineers to be "stationed at West Point." Jefferson, furthermore, was given the power to appoint all its officers. Among the Corps's most important missions was to "constitute a military academy"—a duty that would remain the exclusive domain of the engineers for decades to come.

A full quarter century after General Knox had first suggested it, after two presidents had pressed for it and a third had been persuaded of its merits, after many false starts and missteps, the dream of so many for so long had at last become reality. The date Jefferson signed the vital piece of legislation, March 16, 1802, has forever after been celebrated as the birthday of the United States Military Academy.

Cannon captured during various wars are on display at Trophy Point. These cannon from the Mexican War (1846–48) were sent to West Point by Winfield Scott, commander of U.S. forces in Mexico. Scott gave significant credit for the U.S. victory to the West Pointers on his staff, an important boast to the fledgling military academy.

Major Jonathan Williams, who carried the titles of both chief engineer of the Corps and superintendent of the Academy, was given a faculty of two professors and a minuscule budget to procure textbooks and classroom supplies. He immediately faced a multitude of problems. Classes were held in a cramped, two-story building that dated from the Revolutionary War. Cadets lived in drafty, wooden barracks that were just as old and almost impossible to heat. The students themselves varied in age from as young as ten to well into their thirties—one middle-aged man arrived with his wife and children in tow. Some cadets possessed college degrees and experience in law or other professional fields, while others—undoubtedly of good Jeffersonian-Republican stock—had only a primary education and a rudimentary grasp of writing and arithmetic. Worse still, they arrived unannounced, with appointment letters in hand, at any time throughout the year.

Major Jonathan Williams was appointed by President Thomas Jefferson as the first superintendent of the Corps of Engineers at West Point in 1801.

With the great disparity in ages and prior schooling among his cadets, and with only two instructors to teach them, Williams faced a demoralizing situation. Classes inevitably moved at the pace of the slowest students. Nor could cadets who wished to study on their own find much help in the academy's paltry library. Williams could not add geometry to the curriculum without drawing instruments, and his simple requisition for twelve inexpensive sets took months to fill.

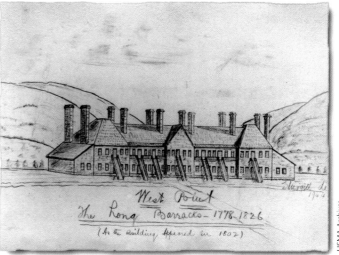

The War Department turned down the superintendent's appeals for more and newer texts on the specious grounds that scientific knowledge was changing so rapidly that the books would be out of date by the time they arrived. Discouraging as all this was, Williams counseled one of his officers never to "lose sight of our leading star, which is not a little mathematical School, but a great national establishment to turn out characters which in the course of time shall equal any in Europe."

Long Barracks, built as part of the defense fortifications during the Revolutionary War, served as early cadet housing after the establishment of the Academy. It was destroyed by a fire in 1826.

The superintendent did enjoy one success during this period: Congress approved his petition to hire two additional instructors—for French and drawing—with the admonition to steer clear of "intemperate men, foreigners, or men far advanced in years." The staff and students, meanwhile, settled into a routine. Classes were held six days a week from 9:00 A.M. to 2:00 P.M.; on four afternoons a week, the cadets would gather for outdoor sessions to learn skills such as surveying and map drawing.

West Point Museum Collections, USMA

Above: *Joseph Swift, shown here in an 1829 painting by Thomas Sully, was the first graduate of the U.S. Military Academy.* Below: *Although a civilian at the time, Swift chose to carry this U.S. Model 1842 holster pistol. It was once considered the finest issue military pistol in the world.*

West Point Museum
Collections, USMA

Less than six months after Jefferson signed it into law, the U.S. Military Academy graduated its first cadets. With no formal requirements or procedures in place, a cadet could take the examinations whenever Williams and his instructors felt he was ready. On September 1, 1802, two cadets faced a barrage of questions on the subjects of mathematics, natural philosophy (or physics, as it is now called), and the theories of fortification construction and artillery usage. Both answered to the satisfaction of their professors, and Cadet Joseph Swift—the same "mutinous rascal" who had chased and threatened his first math instructor—entered the annals of West Point history as the Academy's first graduate. Simon M. Levy became the second—and first Jewish cadet—so honored. They were commissioned second lieutenants and remained at West Point as members of the garrison.

But despite this significant milestone, Williams grew increasingly disenchanted with the government's neglect of and the country's indifference toward West Point. The threat of war had dissipated; Congress and the general public turned their attention to other matters, such as the vast territory west of the Mississippi that President Jefferson had just purchased from France. "The military academy, as it now stands," Williams glumly wrote the secretary of war, "is like a foundling, barely existing among the mountains, and nurtured at a distance out of sight, and almost unknown to its legitimate parents."

One of his school's most fundamental problems, in Williams's view, was its location. "The military academy is at present in a miserable state," he grumbled, "resulting from an Absurd Condition in its original creation *'that it shall be stationed at West Point'*." Throughout his tenure he campaigned long and hard to have the Academy moved to Washington, but Congress never approved the transfer. Williams, now a lieutenant colonel, grew so fed up with the state of affairs that he resigned his commission in June 1803.

His presence was missed; Lieutenant Swift wrote: "Colonel Williams had been the friend and advisor of every one of us." His successor, Major Decius

Wadsworth, fared no better in getting remedial action from Congress or the War Department. Furthermore, long and frequent absences from West Point in connection with his duties as chief engineer left little time to attend to his superintendent role. One cadet sent a pleading letter to Williams: "Never was West Point so much in want of you as at this moment. Everything is going to ruin, Morals and knowledge thrive little and courts-martial and flogging prevail." By 1805 the new superintendent, having spent the winter (as he termed it) "buried alive in snow at West Point," was ordered to New Orleans and tendered his resignation. A personal appeal from Jefferson finally convinced Williams to return.

Reform and reorganization at the Academy still proceeded at a snail's pace; an 1806 graduate referred to it as "the elementary school at West Point." In 1808 Congress authorized an expansion of West Point's student body from forty-four to two hundred. But appointments from the War Department lagged far behind; two years later a mere forty-seven cadets were enrolled. "I totally despair," Williams lamented, "of any alteration that will raise the Academy to that state which the honor of the nation and the advantage of the Army indispensably require." One important proviso for admission was finally standardized—new cadets had to be between fourteen and twenty-one years of age—but

In the early years of the Military Academy, there was no regular graduation schedule. The first two graduates attended for less than a year. Today the Academy graduates nearly a thousand new officers annually, each of whom completes a rigorous four-year study program.

© Ted Spiegel

the Academy remained an overlooked, dilapidated institution when the United States found itself at war with Great Britain in 1812.

At the onset of the war, the engineers and instructors stationed at West Point were reassigned to other posts. Colonel Williams requested command of a fortification he had designed and built in New York Harbor. When the War Department turned him down, he resigned once more in a huff. After a decade of Williams's unswerving devotion to the school he had guided through its trying infancy, the Academy and its handful of cadets were left without a faculty or a superintendent.

Meanwhile, Congress and President James Madison were working frantically to increase the regular army's strength from eleven to twenty-four regiments, while at the same time issuing a call for thirty thousand volunteer troops and asking the individual states to supply eighty thousand militia. To fill the swelling officer corps needed to command this huge force, the Military Academy had produced a mere eighty-nine graduates.

Congress at last acted to rectify its long-standing apathy toward West Point. A reorganization bill, passed in April 1812, increased the number of cadets to 250. It also authorized permanent faculty chairs in mathematics, natural and experimental philosophy, French, the art of engineering, and drawing, so that cadets might "receive a regular degree from an academic staff." To provide them a proper military foundation, cadets would be formed into companies and participate annually in a three-month encampment to learn "all of the duties of a private, a noncommissioned officer, and officer." Congress also appropriated twenty-five thousand dollars for physical improvements to West Point and to build a proper library.

> " [NEVER] LOSE SIGHT OF OUR LEADING STAR, WHICH IS NOT A LITTLE MATHEMATICAL SCHOOL, BUT A GREAT NATIONAL ESTABLISHMENT TO TURN OUT CHARACTERS WHICH IN THE COURSE OF TIME SHALL EQUAL ANY IN EUROPE. "
>
> — SUPERINTENDENT JONATHAN WILLIAMS

To oversee these changes and replace the retired Williams, former cadet—and now colonel—Joseph Swift was chosen as the new superintendent. The war years from 1812 to 1815 were a hectic time at West Point. Cadets were summoned to active duty as soon as they had mastered the barest rudiments of military science; most spent less than a year at the Academy. Wartime demands also kept Swift away from West Point almost constantly. In his absence he designated Captain Alden Partridge, professor of engineering, as de facto superintendent. Meanwhile a building boom, fueled by the congressional appropriation,

Opposite: A cadet company proudly displays its guidon during parade review.

© Ted Spiegel

produced the Academy's first permanent structures: a barracks, a mess hall and kitchen, and a two-story edifice that housed a classroom and laboratory, as well as the library and chapel. Setting a tradition that has continued to this day, many buildings were situated on the southern fringe of the grassy Plain, and many were made of local gray granite.

The War of 1812 ended after three years of inconclusive conflict, and in its aftermath Secretary of War James Monroe acted quickly to correct one problem that had plagued the Academy since its inception. Realizing that the chief engineer of the Corps had too many responsibilities to devote sufficient time to the school, he established a separate position of "Permanent Superintendent" who "shall have exclusive control of the Institution and all those connected with it." The first officer to hold this title was Captain Alden Partridge, while General Swift retained his post as chief engineer.

The new superintendent was a complex and quirky man. He had breezed through final exams in 1806 after less than a year at the Academy, so impressing Colonel Williams and his instructors that he received a first lieutenant's commission. As a professor, and then as acting superintendent, he had shown himself to be energetic and utterly devoted to the Academy. But he was also scheming, spiteful, and extremely vain. He never appeared in public in anything less than full-dress uniform, complete with sword and sash, yet his tastes were otherwise unpretentious and his quarters downright austere.

To a man, the professors and officers of the garrison loathed Partridge. He never solicited advice or delegated authority, and he brooked no criticism of any decision he made. His meddling with professors' course outlines and teaching methods was so invasive that one complained they had "no rights or privileges, even in their own departments."

The cadets, on the other hand, adored their superintendent even though Partridge was a stickler for discipline. He would prowl the barracks most evenings to make sure everyone was studying diligently. He tolerated no vulgar language, gambling, or "immoral conduct" among his charges. Partridge punished the most serious infractions of Academy regulations by confining the offender—never for more than half an hour—in the Black Hole, a "filthy and uncomfortable" subterranean chamber on the grounds of old Fort Clinton. But he also took all his meals with them in the mess hall, and made them feel a valuable part of the institution with a weekly briefing and review of events or developments that affected them and their school.

In winter Partridge would enliven artillery practice by turning the school's fieldpiece toward the Hudson and letting students skip cannonballs off the ice. He even made the almost constant drilling enjoyable by forming the cadet companies into miniature armies to act out great battles from history. While the cadets marched,

In 1802 the Academy graduated only two cadets. Today the Academy graduates about 1,000 cadets annually.

© Ted Spiegel

THE GENESIS OF THE
LONG GRAY LINE

Since switching to gray wool in the early 1800s, the basic design of the cadet uniform has remained largely the same. Above: Cadet Edgar S. Hawkins, a watercolor by an unknown artist (circa 1820), is one of the earliest depictions of a cadet in uniform. Below: The Long Gray Line today.

© Ted Spiegel

*I*n 1810 Major Jonathan Williams persuaded the War Department to issue the following directive: "A uniform shall be established by the Superintendent, with the approbation of the Secretary of War, for all Cadets attached to the Academy, without regard to their respective corps." It took four years, however, for the army's inspector general to prepare regulations describing that uniform. They read in part: "Coat, blue cloth, single breasted, standing collar, eight buttons in front, six in rear, one on each side of the collar, with one blind buttonhole, and one on each cuff." Headgear would consist of a "round hat, cockade with gilt eagle and loop," and every cadet would be issued a "cut and thrust sword in a frog belt worn under the coat."

By the time these instructions reached West Point, the regular army—greatly expanded during the War of 1812—had consumed all the blue fabric available in America. Consequently, cadets were issued gray woolen uniforms designed by Superintendent Alden Partridge in the summer of 1814. Two years later General Swift proposed that this shade be made permanent because "the price of the uniform $18 to $20 better suits the finance of the Cadets than one of blue would." A popular legend maintains the color was chosen to commemorate Winfield Scott's brigade, which wore gray militia uniforms in its victory over British forces in the Battle of Chippewa. In fact, the decision was based solely on cost and availability.

The distinctive gray uniform so closely identified with West Point has undergone many alterations over the years, but the original design is still plainly evident when today's Corps of Cadets marches across the parade ground. And contemporary cadets can no doubt still commiserate with their early-nineteenth-century counterparts—early members of the "Long Gray Line"—who composed the following verse:

> Your coat is made, you button it, give one spasmodic cough, And do not draw another breath until you take it off!

Partridge would provide a running commentary on strategy and tactics, giving them the first and only taste of military history they would receive during their tenure at West Point.

Partridge also instituted many aspects of cadet life that are still recognizable today. He was the first to clothe them in gray uniforms, which he designed himself. He also introduced a strictly regimented daily routine that accounted for the cadets' every waking hour. It began with 6:00 A.M. roll call, followed by an inspection of quarters. At 7:00 the cadets would march to the mess hall for breakfast, which, like all meals, they would eat in "utmost order and silence." Mathematics class lasted from 8:00 to 11:00; then came two hours of French instruction. Dinner, the day's main meal, was served from 1:00 to 2:00. Engineering and drawing classes were held in the afternoon, followed by drill, study hours, an evening parade, and a light supper.

USMA Archives

Captain Alden Partridge, an 1806 West Point graduate, was the first officer to serve as permanent superintendent of the Military Academy, an administrative change that proved vital for the development of the Academy.

Despite his many innovations and strong dedication to the Academy, Partridge's reign ended ignominiously. His subordinates' bitterness spawned rumors and finally led to allegations of fraud, nepotism, and mismanagement. Partridge responded by arresting all the professors and teaching every class himself. In the end, whether the charges against him were valid, exaggerated, or altogether spurious made little difference; Superintendent Alden Partridge was done in by his own prickly personality and overbearing comportment.

In June 1817 newly elected president James Monroe journeyed to West Point to investigate the matter for himself. What he saw—and heard from the staff—convinced him that Partridge must go, and a replacement was soon named. Owing to the circumstances of his departure, Partridge's positive and lasting contributions to the U.S. Military Academy are often overlooked. But in his favor it must be said that he helped lay the foundation for his illustrious successor.

CHAPTER THREE

1817—1848

A SENSE
of PURPOSE

Of all the illustrious military commanders

and national heroes who have passed through the gates of West Point during the last two

hundred years, only a handful have been commemorated with statues on the school's

hallowed grounds. One of these, which stands on the northern edge of the

Plain overlooking the drill field, bears a short, unequivocal inscription:

FATHER OF THE MILITARY ACADEMY. The name above that reverential epithet

reads simply COLONEL THAYER.

Sylvanus Thayer was not the founder of the Academy—that

honor is more appropriately bestowed on Thomas Jefferson—nor did

he preside over its arduous birth. Rather, he earned the title *father* by

shepherding West Point through its difficult formative years. When Thayer

was named superintendent in 1817, the Military Academy stood in

turmoil, its faculty at war with his predecessor, Alden Partridge, and the

cadets woefully unprepared for the rigors of higher education. When he

left in 1833, West Point was firmly established as an indispensable national institution—as

well as the finest engineering school in the country. He laid the didactic foundation of the

Academy, set down the code of conduct expected of its students, and devised goals for both

that are, for the most part, still in place today. Sylvanus Thayer gave West Point and the

Corps of Cadets a sense of purpose that endured long after he departed.

Born in Massachusetts in 1785, Thayer seemed destined from childhood for a military

life. As a boy he had listened with rapt attention to the Revolutionary War tales of his father

and uncles, all veterans of the Continental Army. Thayer, like Alden Partridge, was an

ardent admirer of Napoleon. As a young man he diligently studied contemporary accounts

As a young lieutenant, Sylvanus Thayer served as a junior officer in the War of 1812. This portrait of the Brevet Brigadier General is by Arthur Dawson.

West Point Museum Collections, USMA

Above: *In 1815 Thayer was sent to France to collect books on military science. These became the core of the Academy's library.* Below: *L'Ecole Polytechnique monument was presented to the Academy in 1919 by cadets of the French school.*

of the great strategist's triumphant campaigns. In 1807, following four years at Dartmouth—where he distinguished himself as an outstanding student and orator—Thayer enrolled at West Point. Not surprisingly, he easily passed the examinations one year later and received his commission as a second lieutenant of engineers.

Lieutenant Thayer competently fulfilled his duties as a junior officer during the War of 1812, but was dismayed by the generally poor showing of his fellow West Point graduates in that conflict. The experience convinced Thayer that America still had a lot to learn from the military experts in Europe. Meanwhile, President Madison and General Swift had independently reached the same conclusion. In 1815 they dispatched Thayer to France with a five-thousand-dollar allowance to purchase textbooks and classroom tools for the Academy. The young lieutenant was also ordered to "prosecute enquiries and examination, calculated for your improvement in the military art. The military schools and work-shops, and arsenals, the canals and harbors, the fortifications, especially those for maritime defense, will claim your particular attention."

Unfortunately for this devotee of Napoleon, Thayer arrived in France three weeks after his hero's downfall at the Battle of Waterloo. In the chaos that followed, military

installations were placed off limits to curious foreign officers, but he was eventually permitted to visit both an artillery school and the premier military academy in the world, the École Polytechnique, which greatly impressed him. In the bookstores of Paris, he also secured about a thousand invaluable tomes—most in French, the language that, he professed, "may be considered as the sole repository of Military science"—as well as some maps and scale models of forts. This treasure trove of scientific and military wisdom was packed up and shipped off to West Point, where it formed the core of the Academy's library.

Thayer remained abroad for almost a year, soaking up as much knowledge from Europe's military establishments and professional officer corps as possible. While

Thayer was still in France, President Madison's successor, James Monroe, selected him to replace the tempestuous Superintendent Partridge. Monroe's secretary of war wrote to Thayer with the fervent hope "that under your auspices, those feuds and dissentions which have so materially injured the institution, and harassed the government will cease; and that the Military Academy will be brought to a degree of perfection corresponding with the views of the government, and the expectations of the public."

Brevet Major Sylvanus Thayer thus became the U.S. Military Academy's fifth superintendent. His first act was to release the professors whom Partridge had placed under arrest. Then, in order to mend fences and restore trust in his office, Thayer courteously requested all faculty members to prepare a comprehensive review of their departments, "specifying the branches to be taught, the time required for each, and the books which shall serve as guides." He studied these reports thoroughly to see how the curriculum might be improved. Thayer already had several reforms in mind based on what he had observed in France, but, heedful of the faculty's feelings, he presented his own plan "not with an idea that the opinions here advanced are the most correct, but with the view to invite a discussion of the subject and to elicit your opinion thereon."

Colonel Sylvanus Thayer, Class of 1808, served as superintendent from 1817 to 1833. He put his mark on the institution to a greater extent than any other individual. This 1843 Robert Weir oil painting is part of the collection at the West Point Museum.

West Point Museum Collections, USMA

The professors, who only a short while before had been under house arrest and forbidden to teach their courses, let alone express any opinions on how those courses should be taught, were astonished and delighted. "This business is new to me," Thayer assured them, "and I rely with pleasure on the superior judgment of the learned professors." Though he was fully qualified to do so, Thayer taught no classes himself; nor did he directly participate in the cadets' military training, as Partridge had done. The staff, grateful for this complete about-face from the hostile attitude of the previous regime, quickly rallied behind the new superintendent.

The cadets, however, were another matter; they resented the new man simply for having replaced their beloved Captain Partridge. Once, when Thayer offered career guidance to a graduating cadet, the young man brusquely snapped, "Major Thayer, when I want your advice I'll ask you for it!" Thayer made no attempt to coddle the cadets or curry favor. Quite the contrary, one of his first directives was to order examinations for every student—which he conducted personally—to assess both their academic standing and their character.

Many cadets, derisively known as "Uncle Sam's bad bargains," had lingered at West Point for years under Partridge's tutelage without making any discernible progress toward graduation. Thayer peremptorily dismissed forty-three of them, "most of whom are deficient in natural abilities and all are destitute of those qualities which would encourage a belief that they could be advanced through the four years' course of study. The public money would be wasted, therefore, by retaining them here any longer." By this one act alone, the new superintendent made it obvious to everyone that he meant business.

Another episode gave further indication, if any was needed, of Thayer's commitment to rigorous, objective standards without regard to personal feelings or political repercussions. West Point's first foreign exchange students, two brothers from Chile, had been admitted to the Academy under the patronage of a high-ranking American naval officer. But judging the two by the same exacting, unbiased criteria he applied to the rest of the Corps of Cadets, Thayer found both to be "extremely deficient in the first rudiments of education, reading, writing, and orthography [letters and spelling]" and dismissed them without further ado.

Even if the new superintendent did not immediately win his cadets' affection, he undeniably impressed them with his bearing and integrity. "His object was to make [cadets] gentlemen and soldiers," one admitted. "And he illustrated in his person the great object he sought to accomplish." Every inch a professional soldier, Thayer always dressed impeccably and carried himself with a natural air of authority. With his Dartmouth education and his military experience, he could converse easily and knowledgeably on a wide variety of subjects with professors or visiting dignitaries. "In expressing his ideas, his voice was low, distinct and very impressive," one such visitor marveled, "and when he spoke all present would listen with rapt attention." One of Thayer's graduates noted admiringly that "his comprehensive mind embraced principles and details more strongly than any man I ever knew."

USMA Archives

The section system consisting of small groups of cadets studying together according to ability and performance was one of Thayer's innovations. Here a cadet section marcher reports the roll in his Civil and Military Engineering Class (circa 1903).

A lifelong bachelor, it was clear to instructors and students alike that the Academy served not only as his home, but also as his family and the driving force in his life. So pervasive was the power of Thayer's presence that cadets supposed "his eye was ever on them, both in their rooms and abroad, both in their studies and on parade." He knew every one of them by name, how each stood with his course work, and whether he had recently been cited for any rules violations.

USMA Archives

The superintendent's house, completed in 1820, has been modified many times over the years. Above: As it appeared circa 1870. Below: Cadets march before it today.
© Ted Spiegel

In matters of discipline Thayer was exceedingly strict: "Gentlemen must learn," he opined, "it is only their province to listen and obey." He issued some two hundred new regulations that covered every aspect—and every waking moment—of a cadet's daily life, as well as the care and maintenance of his belongings and the proper organization of his quarters, which consisted of a ten-by-twelve-foot room shared by five cadets. One order, posted on the door of every barracks room, was copied down verbatim by Cadet William Dutton, who forwarded it to his incredulous cousin (see sidebar on page 34).

In a letter to his brother, Cadet Dutton also left a thoroughly unromanticized account of the daily routine as stipulated by Thayer: "At 5 A.M. which is ½ an hour after the morning gun, the drums are beat by the barracks, & the cry grows—'fall in there,' when we all have to be in the ranks or be reported. The roll is then called, we go to our rooms & have 15 minutes to roll up our blankets put them up, wash, clean the room etc., when everything must be in order." At that point another drumbeat called the bleary-eyed cadets to breakfast. "We then march to the mess hall, & if one speaks, raises his hand, looks to the right or left (which is the case on all parade) we are reported indeed we are reported for everything. . . . When we arrive at the tables, the command is given 'take seats,' & then such a scrambling you never saw. . . . We have to eat as fast as we can, & before we get enough, the command is given 'Squad rise.'"

A full schedule of classes, interrupted only by the main meal of the day at midday, was followed by that never-ending staple of all cadets' existence: "We have to drill twice a day, & a good many faint away," Dutton avowed. "It is terrible, but I like the whole of it, after we have marched from tea [the light evening meal], we stay in our rooms till ½ hour past 9 when we can go to bed if we choose, & at taps at 10 every light must be out & after that the inspector happens in all times of night."

Even the Sabbath had its own attendant miseries. "I have just got back from church, after hearing a rather dry sermon," wrote Cadet George Cullum, who pined for the Sunday services in his hometown. "If I had not there the pleasure of hearing a good sermon, I had at least the pleasure of seeing all my young friends, particularly my female acquaintances; but when I go to church here, I am obliged to sit for two hours on a bench without a back, squeesed [sic] up

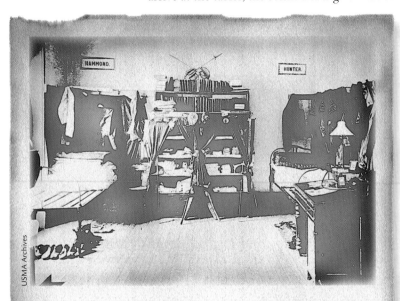

USMA Archives

Bedstead—against door, **Trunks**—under iron bedsteads, **Lamps**—clean on mantel, **Dress Caps**—Neatly arranged behind door, **Looking-Glass**—between washstand & door, **Books**—neatly arranged on shelf farthest from door, **Broom**—Hanging behind door, **Drawing books**—under shelf farthest from door, **Muskets**—in gun rack and locks sprung, **Bayonets** in scabbards, **Accoutrements**—Hanging over muskets, **Sabres**—**Cutlasses &** **swords**—hanging over muskets, **Candle Box**—for scrubbing utensils—Against wall under shelf nearest door, & fire place, **clothes**—neatly hung on pegs over, **bedsteads**—Mattress & Blankets neatly folded, **Orderly Board**—over mantle, **chairs**—when not used under tables—Orderlies of rooms are held responsible for the observance of the above mentioned arrangement. By order of Lieut. E. J. Steptoe—1st Lieut. 1st Art. & commd't A compy.

© Robert Stewart

© Ted Spiegel

During his tenure as superintendent, Sylvanus Thayer created rigid requirements to guide nearly every aspect of cadet life. Cadets were permitted only certain items in their rooms, and each item had an assigned place. Such limitations have largely remained in place through the years.

Opposite:
An 1877 cadet room.

Top: *Today cadets continue to adhere to strict rules of cleanliness and organization.*

Bottom: *A replica of typical cadet quarters in the 1920s.*

among a parcel of Cadets, and squeesed up more with my belts, as we have all to wear our side arms to church."

Most of Superintendent Thayer's rules dealt with what constituted unacceptable cadet behavior: "Games of chance are strictly forbidden," read one, which further specified that "any Cadet who shall be convicted of Card Playing either at his Quarters or elsewhere, or of having Cards in his possession, of procuring them or causing them to be procured" would be immediately dismissed. "The practice of chewing, snuffing, & smoking tobacco," decreed another of Thayer's orders— issued, far ahead of its time, in 1823—"being deemed pernicious to the health of the students of the Military Academy, and as being altogether unnecessary & inconsistent with a due respect to economy is hereby forbidden and prohibited."

The ban on tobacco apparently did not impede another nasty habit of that time, for a separate regulation specified: "The practice among the Cadets of spitting on the floors of the section rooms and Academies must immediately cease. The rooms have all been

> " AT 5 A.M. . . . THE CRY GROWS—'FALL IN THERE,' WHEN WE ALL HAVE TO BE IN THE RANKS OR BE REPORTED. THE ROLL IS THEN CALLED, WE GO TO OUR ROOMS & HAVE 15 MINUTES TO ROLL UP OUR BLANKETS PUT THEM UP, WASH, CLEAN THE ROOM ETC., WHEN EVERYTHING MUST BE IN ORDER. "
>
> — CADET WILLIAM DUTTON

A "Minute Caller" alerts cadets to prepare for formation.
© Bob Krist

furnished with spit boxes, and the instructors will be vigilant that this order is duly observed." Other prohibited activities included drinking, brawling, dueling, wearing civilian clothes, leaving barracks rooms without permission, writing articles about the Academy for publication, or petitioning the secretary of war.

The most common punishments for disciplinary infractions that did not warrant dismissal were confinement to quarters, reduction in rank, extra tours of guard duty, and extra drill. Thayer's stringent parameters caused near riots among the Corps of Cadets on occasion, but the superintendent never wavered in his commitment to order and obedience. Even the most livid cadets could see that, unlike Partridge, Thayer was absolutely impartial in administering justice. "Favoritism is now banished," wrote one professor, "and the road opened for the advancement of Merit, whether it be found in the son of a beggar, or a King." Moreover, Thayer was capable, on occasion, of leniency or even of reversing a decision, if the offending party showed proper remorse and a genuine pledge to atone. "Cadet Southland being sensible of his error in refusing to recite to Cadet Washington [a cadet instructor]," he wrote concerning one such incident in 1820, "and

Cadets McNutt, Kennon, Fish, and Carleton pose for a photo portraying numerous regulations violations. This photo originally appeared in the 1881 class album.
USMA Archives

"FAVORITISM IS NOW BANISHED, AND THE ROAD OPENED FOR THE ADVANCEMENT OF MERIT, WHETHER IT BE FOUND IN THE SON OF A BEGGAR, OR A KING."

— A WEST POINT PROFESSOR

having promised future obedience, the order directing his dismission is hereby countermanded."

With the faculty's staunch support and the War Department's blessing, Thayer embarked on his sweeping reform program. First, he abolished the practice of cadets reporting at any time during the year; henceforth all incoming cadets would report in June so that each year's class would begin together and progress collectively. Furthermore, all students, without exception, would remain at West Point for a four-year program of study and military training. No longer would cadets be examined and commissioned—as he had been—whenever their professors felt they were ready.

During the summer when classes were not in session, Thayer set up an encampment of canvas tents on the grassy Plain so that his students might become acquainted with the rigors of a soldier's life in the field. Cadets carried bedding from their barracks rooms to sleep on, but cots were forbidden. The only nod to comfort was the wooden floors Thayer finally authorized in 1829, which, according to one grateful cadet, "keep us perfectly guarded from the dampness of the ground." To supervise the training of the Corps of

Summer encampments on the Plain provided a break from the normal class routine.

USMA Archives

Cadets, now more than two hundred strong, he appointed a regular army officer to the newly created position of commandant of cadets.

Incoming cadets faced an immediate shock: "The first day after my arrival," Abner Hetzel wrote to his father in June 1823, "I was taken out to drill & sure you never saw a more awkward creature in your life than I was or appeared to be. Indeed every new cadet appears to have the gyves [shackles] on." After two weeks of drilling and remedial academic instruction for the benefit of those with little or no formal education, the cadets undertook their first test. Hetzel explained, "I was examined for admission into the Institution last Saturday in Co. with nearly 100 others." To his great relief, he was accepted, but, as he told his father, "4 out of 9 were rejected that came up with me on the Steam Boat, one of whom came from Louisiana, a distance of 2300 miles. We then received our Knapsacks, pack'd up our clothing & marched into Camp."

Once the new cadets, or plebes, were installed in their tents, the commandant and his assistants, known as tactical officers, introduced them to the more prosaic features of an army

From their very first day at West Point, cadets quickly learn to follow strict military standards.

Preceding page: Part of the Reception Day (R-Day) experience includes learning proper military stance and courtesies.

© Robert Stewart

Right: *New plebes circa the 1920s arrive via steamboat.*

USMA Archives

Below: *Plebes circa 1990 line up to start R-Day.*

© Ted Spiegel

career. "I was obliged to stand guard 4 hours in the Day & 4 hours in the night," Cadet John Pope grumbled in a letter to his mother. "I tell you about 3 o'clock at night walking Post both Cold & Dark and raining I thought of my Dear Mother & home & wished that I were with them." Pope, who would later become a general in the Civil War, found daytime duty even more enervating. "The skin is coming off my face up to my nose on account of standing Guard yesterday for four hours during the most intense heat and we are obliged to wear those tall bell crowned leather Caps which with the brass trimmings weigh about 5 Pounds and hurt my head extremely and the rim also coming just to the nose."

Cadet Benjamin Latrobe recalled years later, "How well do I remember the parallel lines of shallow trenches, twenty-eight inches apart, on the east side of North Barracks, over which the squads were marched back and forth, again and again, until they were supposed to be able to step that distance uniformly in the daily drill." Regarding his own progress, Latrobe noted, "it took a good deal, no doubt, to bring me up to the cadet pattern, and the work was done by those who, having gone through the mill themselves, seemed to take malicious pleasure in grinding me between the same stones."

Above: An 1828 artillery drill on the Plain, as depicted by George Catlin.
Below: Cadets learn to operate large artillery guns during summer camp in the early 1900s.

Upperclassmen, it seems, could not resist the temptation of having a little fun at the expense of these bewildered neophytes. Cadet George Cullum told a friend, "I wish you could be here one night when I am on guard to visit with me some of those raw plebes on post. I can assure you I have some rare sport with them. Sometimes we get into Fort Clinton which is close by their line of posts, and flash powder at them or wrap ourselves in sheets and then run across the posts on our hands and feet muttering some undiscovered language, which they, poor simpletons, take to be ghosts or the devil himself."

Still, there was nothing approaching the type of improper and debasing behavior called hazing that in later years came to plague the Academy. Half a century after he graduated, one West Pointer remembered that "the name cadet, whether belonging to the last admitted plebe or to the graduating first class man, was honored by all and indignity offered to the former would have been resented as even, by the Corps as one offered to the latter."

The plebes did find some aspects of the summer encampment to be quite exhilarating, if also a little startling. "Immediately after guard mounting we had artillery drill," one wrote to his hometown minister, "we had six large brass field pieces, at first it used to almost deafen me, it would have astonished you I think to see little boys not 5 feet high touching off a large cannon, and performing all the duties necessary to man a piece."

Speaking with the voice of experience, Cadet Cullum noted that the drill "affords us no small quantity of amusement. Never being accustomed to hear so many pieces discharged at once so near them they make as much fuss as though they had an arm or two shot off."

Superintendent Thayer also instituted a chain of command within the cadet companies, with a captain, three lieutenants, a first sergeant, four sergeants, and four corporals chosen from among the upperclassmen. Chevrons—gold lace for officers and yellow cloth for sergeants and corporals—on the cadets' uniform sleeves denoted rank. This not only instilled pride in the recipients but also gave them real responsibilities and invaluable experience in the practical matters of drilling troops and commanding small units during tactical exercises.

Only Third Class, or second-year, cadets were exempt from the summer encampment. It was the only time under Thayer's system that students were allowed to leave West Point on vacation during the entire four years—and they treasured it. "Every moment is nearer than the preceding to that happy time known as furlough time," Cadet James Schureman wrote to his sister; "it is a period ever welcome to a cadet, its joys constitute his dreams by night, his thoughts by day . . . it is liberty sweetened by confinement, and ease enhanced by previous labours. Long and ardently have I wished for that happy moment to arrive when I can say farewell O West Point with all thy grandeur and thy halls of science and to say mind rest for a season from thy laborious occupation, home and friends are far more endearing than you all."

When cadets returned to their studies in the fall, they found a standardized curriculum—a practice that had begun under Partridge but was carried further by Thayer. All members of any given year's class, for example, would take the same courses at the same time. And

This lithograph by Seth Eastman from the West Point Museum Collection depicts cadets' summer encampment in 1835. Situated on the northern edge of the Plain overlooking the Hudson River is the West Point Hotel, built in 1829. The old hotel was finally torn down in 1932.

anything less than total diligence to one's lessons would not be tolerated. "When it shall appear," Thayer decreed, "that any cadet has been habitually inattentive to his studies, he will be struck from the rolls of the military academy."

In order to keep class sizes small and to provide an inducement for top-quality upperclassmen, Thayer inaugurated the system of using cadet instructors to supplement the seven-man, full-time faculty—one of the many innovations that remained in place for decades after his departure. To be appointed an acting assistant professor was not only "considered an honorable distinction," according to Thayer's own regulations, but also provided tangible rewards. Cadet instructors received an additional ten dollars a month, were excused from certain duties, including marching to class, and were authorized to wear three rows of fourteen buttons on their uniforms instead of the usual eight buttons per row. There were also advantages to rooming with these chosen few: "Fortunately I live with a Cadet Professor," George Cullum wrote, "who is entitled to a light after taps (10 O'clock) by which I am very glad to profit until about 12, as it requires all of that time for me to get my lessons."

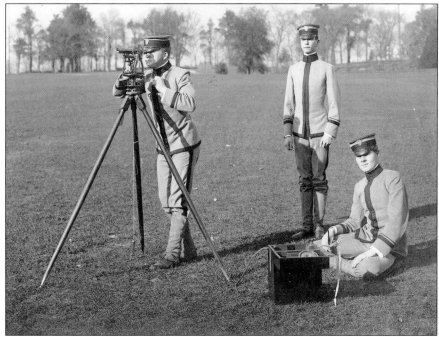

USMA Archives

Thayer's curriculum placed the greatest emphasis on two courses: French was indispensable in view of the fact that so many military textbooks and treatises were available only in that language, while mathematics was even more important in his eyes as the foundation of an engineering degree. The new superintendent was quickly apprised of the cadets' deficiencies in the latter field by his professor of engineering, Claude Crozet. A graduate of the École Polytechnique and a veteran of Napoleon's army, Crozet had arrived at West Point in 1815 prepared to impart the technical aspects of engineering to eager young American minds. "The surprise of the French engineer instructed in the Polytechnique," wrote one of his students, "may well be imagined when he commenced giving his classes certain problems and instructions, which not one of them could comprehend or perform."

Compounding the problem was Crozet's rudimentary grasp of English and his thick accent, which, as another cadet recalled, necessitated that "instruction had to be conveyed

Above: *Training cadets to draw maps and sketches of terrain and fortifications, along with classical drawings, has long been a part of the Academy's curriculum.* Below: *This drawing of the* Head of Minerva *was done by Jefferson Davis (Class of 1828) when he was a cadet.*

through the medium of Cadets who understood something of French." The frustrated professor soon came to rely on visual aids. One of his colleagues observed that concepts and exercises were "drawn and demonstrated on the blackboard, by the Professor, then drawn and demonstrated by the pupils, and then accurately copied into permanent drawings."

Both Thayer and Crozet had to face the harsh reality that many cadets arriving at West Point possessed only a rudimentary background in simple arithmetic. Their solution was to institute a progressive four-year course of study in mathematics, leading from algebra, geometry, and trigonometry to calculus and, ultimately, in a cadet's final year, to engineering itself. "We have just finished our course for this year and are now reviewing, we went as far as Spherical Projections in Descriptive Geometry," Cadet William Frazer proudly reported to his brother, "it is a study which is studied no other place but here." In this way the Military Academy transformed itself into the premier school of engineering in the entire country.

Other fields of study, including analytical and topographical drawing, physics, chemistry, mineralogy, rhetoric, and political science, rounded out the cadets' education. Cadet James Shureman gave his sister a vivid account of physics class: "We have had some most beautiful experiments. I took an electric shock a few days ago which nearly shook me to pieces. The electric machine which we use . . . is perhaps about as good an one [sic] as any in the United States."

Cadet George Cullum waxed eloquent on the joys of the topographical drawing course: "I have just returned from a hard morning's work, of surveying. I have been taking a plan of the point, for the sake of a little practice and still more for some fresh air. It is delightful working on the field instead of on the blackboard, particularly as we sometimes have a peep at some of the fair sex, when taking the positions of their dwellings."

A distinguished guest was once conducted to the library to view some samples of the cadets' work in drawing class. "There were perhaps four hundred on the greatest variety of subjects, heads, figures, landscapes, topographical drawings," he observed, "and though each cadet was obliged to produce his specimens and have them hung with his

WEST POINT'S FAVORITE WATERING HOLE

Benny Havens, Oh!
(sung to the tune of "The Wearin' of the Green")

Come, fill your glasses, fellows, and stand up in a row,
To singing sentimentally, we're going for to go;
In the army there's sobriety, promotion's very slow
So we'll sing our reminiscences of Benny Havens, oh!

Oh! Benny Havens, oh!—oh! Benny Havens, oh!
So we'll sing our reminiscences of Benny Havens, oh!

In 1824 an Irishman named Benny Havens opened a tavern near Buttermilk Falls, a little more than a mile south of the Academy grounds. Cadets were soon beating a path between their barracks and Benny's door. Sneaking out under cover of darkness and dodging sentries, generations of cadets made the pilgrimage to Benny Havens to enjoy a home-cooked meal and, more often than not, something a bit stronger to fortify their spirits.

Benny and his wife made the cadets feel welcome, offering a sympathetic ear and liberal credit; they frequently accepted items such as blankets in trade to settle a tab. If a cadet returned from his summer furlough with a barrel of whiskey, Benny would store it for him and pour a dram whenever the young man stopped by. And if tactical officers approached, Benny would hustle his young customers to safety out the back door.

Buckwheat cakes and roast turkey would have been sufficient enticement to cadets accustomed to drab mess-hall fare, but Benny also offered a special concoction known as a hot flip. He would mix well-beaten eggs, sweetened and spiced, with ale in an earthen-ware jug, then plunge a hot poker into the liquid, giving it a "delicious caramel-like flavor."

For fifty years Benny Havens was the bane of West Point's superintendents—and a cherished sanctuary for its students, who ran great risks to enjoy its convivial atmosphere. In 1825 Cadet Jefferson Davis was caught red handed in the tavern. At his court-martial, he claimed in his defense that he had only been drinking beer, which he did not believe to be a liquor. Convicted nonetheless, Davis was dismissed, but—like so many cadets of that time—was immediately reinstated. Cadet Edgar Allan Poe also numbered among the regular customers. He later wrote that Benny "was the sole congenial soul in the entire God-forsaken place."

While visiting a cadet friend in 1838, an army doctor named Lucius O'Brien spent several happy evenings at Benny Havens. In tribute, he wrote an ode of appreciation to his fellow Irishman, the first verse of which is printed above. The Corps of Cadets adopted the song as its unofficial anthem, and, over the years, more than sixty verses have been added.

Above: Benjamin Havens, by John W. Scott (circa 1870), shows the man who ran the infamous local tavern that was a favorite of AWOL cadets. Below: The escapades at the tavern came to be known to succeeding generations of cadets long after its doors closed—just after the Civil War.

name on them, there was hardly an ordinary piece among them, and not a single bad one." This achievement was all the more remarkable, considering "the amount of instruction and practice allowed them is not great—about two hours a day for not exceeding sixteen months."

Twice a year, in January and June, Thayer conducted examinations in which professors would grill cadets before the Board of Visitors, a creation of the War Department that was intended to keep Washington abreast of developments at far-off West Point. The board consisted of "five gentlemen versed in military and other science" and, over the years, included such distinguished members as statesman and military hero Sam Houston, Governor Dewitt Clinton of New York, and George Ticknor, president of Harvard.

Board members were, almost without exception, thoroughly impressed by what they saw. "The introduction of the analytical method into the course of Natural and Experimental Philosophy [physics] and into the preparatory course of Mathematics," one of their reports stated effusively, "in consequence will probably form an era in the public education of the United States." The board also commended "the manner and decorum of cadets at meals," and noted that "their deportment to each other has been altered since the adoption of regular reports." As to giving due credit for these progressive measures, "the

Superintendent Thayer revitalized the Academy's Board of Visitors. This drawing depicts a typical pre–Civil War examination before the Board.

USMA Archives

Board of Visitors would not fulfill their duty, did they not bear testimony to the improvement which has taken place and is still going on under the direction of the present Superintendent."

George Ticknor, one of the most respected academicians of his time, was moved to comment after witnessing one of Thayer's marathon four-hour examinations that "the young men have that composure which comes from thoroughness, and unite to a remarkable degree, ease with respectful manners towards their teachers." The result of the exam, he added, was "as nearly perfect as anything of the kind ever was."

The cadets' own perception of these affairs was, by and large, a little more jaded: For two weeks prior to his midyear exams, Cadet Cullum declared, "that I scarcely lifted my eyes from my book except to eat and sleep my six hours, and even then after such close application I shuddered to obey the call of 'turn out first section second class.'" And at the conclusion William Dutton sighed, "The long agony is at length over, & it may well be called 'The Agony,' for I have never seen more anguish depicted on the countenances of any than the U.S. Corps of Cadets have manifested."

Cadets study and attend class during the day and devote three hours to study time each evening.
© Bob Krist

On one occasion the president of the Board of Visitors commented that the cadets had performed so flawlessly that it was hard to believe they had no prior knowledge of the questions. Thayer took this off-the-cuff remark as an affront and a challenge, even though the contrite gentleman apologized profusely and insisted he had meant it as a compliment. The superintendent nonetheless immediately reconvened the board and insisted that its members quiz the cadets themselves. "The examination was resumed and continued with the deepest interest," remembered one student, "each

" THE ACADEMY HAS BEEN PLACED IN A STATE OF THE MOST PERFECT ORGANIZATION & EFFICIENCY UNDER [THAYER'S] ADMINISTRATION, & HAS, IN THE LAST FIVE YEARS, GIVEN TO THE ARMY A MAJORITY OF THE GOOD OFFICERS IN IT."

— GENERAL WINFIELD SCOTT

member of the class feeling that an appeal was made to his honor as well as his pride." Once again, the students all passed with flying colors, and the board proffered "the highest compliments."

In recognition of his efforts, Thayer received a promotion to brevet lieutenant colonel on the personal recommendation of General Winfield Scott, who stated that "if

Plebes admire a class ring on "Ring Day." West Point's Class of 1835 originated the class ring custom, now followed at thousands of institutions across the country.

any officer, since the peace, has earned a brevet, Major Thayer is certainly that individual. The Academy has been placed in a state of the most perfect organization & efficiency under his administration, & has, in the last five years, given to the Army a majority of the good officers in it."

The completion of the academic year in June was cause for great celebration at West Point. "The closing up of the Examination was signalized by a display of fire works etc.," Cadet Dutton explained to his brother. "In the P.M. horses were attached to all the cannon on both sides of the plain & the way the cannon balls & bombs flew about was like hail. It seemed as if the earth would open, & the echoing from hill to hill produced an effect. Astonishing. In the evening they sent up rockets from every quarter and the air was full of them, while every now and then large fire bombs were fired from the mortars shaking the earth & lighting the vale as far up as Newburgh & when several hundred feet from the ground would burst & those fragments would again burst with a noise. They then placed candles around a hollow square and danced."

First Class, or fourth-year, cadets who successfully completed their June examinations received commissions, and Thayer next turned his attention to the manner in which these graduates were assigned to the various branches of the army—engineers, artillery, cavalry, and infantry. Before his arrival the system was entirely arbitrary, subject to favoritism and the whim of the superintendent. In what was perhaps Thayer's most significant and lasting reform, he adopted a merit roll for ranking a cadet's performance. He employed a series of strictly objective criteria, and in so doing eliminated any personal judgments—even his own—that might affect an individual's placement.

The heart of the system was an academic grade-point average—3.0 constituted a perfect score, and anything less than 2.0 was considered unsatisfactory—for every course, plus a separate rating for performance on the drill field. Instructors graded every cadet on a daily basis—scores were posted weekly, on Thayer's orders, to foster a sense of competition—and these were added to the marks he received on the semiannual examinations. This cumulative figure could be reduced by demerits for any infraction of Academy regulations or other unacceptable conduct.

The result was a numerical total that impartially determined a cadet's rank within his class. "West Point constitutes the only society of human beings that I have known," one cadet wrote of Thayer's system, "in which the standing of an individual is dependent wholly upon his own merits so far as they can be ascertained without extraneous influence. Birth, avarice, fashion and connections are without effect to determine promotion or punishment." In a letter to his family, another cadet underscored how seriously he and his comrades regarded the merit roll: "I assure you we know that by study and severe application alone we can keep our places. I admire the spirit which pervades the whole class. The common remark is, 'I intend to bone it with all my might.' To bone it means to study hard. Everyone seems determined to rise, or keep his present standing at any rate."

> [I] SHALL PERSEVERE UNTIL I PRODUCE THAT STATE OF MILITARY DISCIPLINE WHICH IS AS INDISPENSABLE IN AN INSTITUTION OF THIS NATURE AS IN A REGULAR ARMY."
>
> —SUPERINTENDENT SYLVANUS THAYER

A page from the merit roll for June 1843.

© Ted Spiegel

Two further incentives spurred the cadets to greater exertions: The secretary of war agreed to Thayer's recommendation to publish the names of the top five cadets in every class in the Army Register in order to "encourage scientific attainments and promote emulous exertions among cadets." Also, under Thayer's system, the highest-ranking cadets were granted commissions in the prestigious Corps of Engineers—by far the choicest duty. Those next on the list became artillery officers, also an agreeable career option, while the rest of the class went to the cavalry and the infantry, which usually meant assignment to some small, forlorn frontier outpost.

Within a few years of Thayer's arrival, the last of the cadets brought in under Alden Partridge had either graduated or departed under other circumstances, thus easing the outright hostility toward the new superintendent that had smoldered within certain disaffected segments of the Corps of Cadets. And while those students who had known no superintendent but Thayer may still not have regarded him with fondness, they nonetheless respected his dynamism, honesty, and fairness. "I am now continuing my course of reformation, have dismissed some cadets, suspended others," Thayer asserted, "and shall persevere until I produce that state of Military discipline which is as indispensable in an institution of this nature as in a regular Army."

The Trophy Point Amphitheatre provides a scenic backdrop for USMA Band performances.
© Ted Spiegel

But at the same time, he also took steps to boost the cadets' morale and esprit de corps, including making effective use of the USMA band. "We have the best band of musick [*sic*] in the United States," boasted one cadet in a letter to a friend, "which keeps a fellows spirits up." Another commented on "how

sweet after poring for a week over a dry mechanics or optics does it fall on the ear." The straitlaced Thayer then provided his charges with a further surprise: "The superintendent allowed our fencing master [Pierre Thomas] to give dancing lessons, and on the days and evenings to which we were allowed to go we had a jolly time."

One novice dance student noted that an epidemic downriver proved to be a stroke of luck for the lonely cadets: "The Cholera in New York has driven legions of girls here who generally, if they are not true orthodox or cripples, attend our cotillion parties very willingly." Thayer was evidently delighted with the results; in 1823 he contracted the services of a well-known dancing instructor from Boston to properly tutor the cadets during summer encampment, thus establishing a precedent of mandatory dance lessons for incoming cadets during plebe summer that continued right up to World War II.

The U.S. Military Academy Band is the U.S. Army's oldest active band and the oldest unit at West Point.

Thayer also arranged excursions to large cities throughout the Northeast during the summer encampment. On these occasions the entire Corps of Cadets, decked out in their striking gray uniforms, would parade through the streets to the strains of martial music and the wild accolades of the crowds. As a way of generating positive publicity for the Academy, this initiative was a stroke of genius; Thayer knew that his cadets could outmarch any local militia unit in the country.

For the 1821 summer outing, the Corps boarded a steamboat at the small dock below the ruins of old Fort Clinton

and sailed up the Hudson to Albany. There, they disembarked and marched some 170 miles through Massachusetts to Boston, cheers echoing off the storefronts lining the main street of every small town along the route. They received an even more enthusiastic reception from the urbane residents of Boston, who presented them with a flag—the Corps of Cadets' first—as a gift. Tired from their long trek but filled with pride, the cadets made excursions to

This fanciful 1852 drawing depicts a sentry waltzing away from his sentry box during summer camp.

West Point cadets make an impressive showing at the St. Louis Exposition in 1904.

USMA Archives

Harvard College, Bunker Hill, and nearby Quincy to pay a formal visit on the aged former president John Adams. "I congratulate you," proclaimed the man who, even while the Revolutionary War still raged, had foreseen the need for a national military academy, "on the great advantages you possess for attaining eminence in letters and science as well as arms." As the cadets listened in rapt attention, he continued, "These advantages are a precious deposit for which you are responsible to your country."

Until Thayer began these tours, a large majority of the general population was only vaguely aware of West Point's existence, and only a relative handful had ever paid a visit to the historic bastion tucked away in the Hudson Highlands. Now thousands of Americans could see firsthand the kind of poised, dedicated officers being groomed at West Point to lead the nation's armies. "It is scarcely possible for any troops to attain the power of manoeuvring with greater precision," gushed the *North American Review* in 1826. "The institution has acquired a wide and honorable reputation, and is deservedly in favor both with the people and the government."

One result of West Point's heightened public recognition and glowing academic renown was a dramatic upsurge in the demand for admission into the Corps of Cadets. Wealthy families considered it a mark of status to have a scion attend such an elite institution, while those of

more humble origins saw a fantastic opportunity for their sons to gain a top-quality education at no cost. To handle the rising volume of inquiries, Thayer prepared a form letter—later expanded

to several pages—that outlined the entrance requirements and the appointment procedure.

Ever since the Academy's founding in 1802, the president of the United States, with the counsel of his secretary of war, had selected the candidates for admission to West Point. Indeed, that had been a central element of Jefferson's plan when he signed the Academy into law, as it allowed him to stock the cadet ranks with like-minded Republicans and thereby reduce the influence of elitist Federalists in the army.

Subsequent presidents had also used cadet appointments as an instrument of political patronage or, on occasion, as a dispensation to influential friends. But the Academy's growing prestige generated public pressure on the legislative branch for the same kind of favors. Prominent and working-class citizens alike started petitioning their congressional representatives for assistance with admission, finally necessitating a change in the procedure. By 1828 Secretary of War James Barbour could report that "in making selections, I have received, and treated with great respect, the recommendations of the members of

West Point graduates have served the country in a variety of capacities over the last 200 years, as military leaders, engineers, explorers on land and in space, and as leaders in business and government.

© Ted Spiegel

Congress." Barbour claimed that, insofar as it was feasible, he sought to appoint one cadet from every congressional district. This system of congressional nominations thus became an unwritten rule until it was formalized by a legislative act in 1843.

No matter who appointed the incoming candidates, Superintendent Thayer still found that, in any given year, 30—and sometimes as high as 60—percent did not meet the minimum standards for admission. Furthermore, attrition due to academic deficiency or disciplinary offenses over four years eliminated more than half of every class by the time it reached graduation. One problem that had plagued Thayer throughout his tenure was the propensity for presidents and secretaries of war to overrule the superintendent and reinstate cadets whom he had dismissed.

© Bettmann/CORBIS

Although he once supported the Military Academy, as president, Andrew Jackson found himself constantly at odds with Superintendent Thayer. Eventually Thayer resigned rather than risk damage to the institution.

" SYLVANUS THAYER IS A TYRANT! THE AUTOCRAT OF ALL THE RUSSIAS COULDN'T EXERCISE MORE POWER."

— P R E S I D E N T
A N D R E W   J A C K S O N

Thayer's troubles intensified in 1829 when Andrew Jackson took the oath as the nation's seventh president. War hero, militia general, and the first westerner to hold that office, Jackson brought his own brand of government to Washington. Jacksonian Democracy, in its most basic sense, represented an unwavering commitment to social equality and an outright war on privilege. The U.S. Military Academy was an obvious target. Davy Crockett, a fellow Tennessean who had been elected to Congress on Jackson's coattails, introduced legislation to abolish the institution, but the measure did not come close to passage. Jackson's own thoughts are harder to decipher. Two of his nephews had graduated from West Point, and, in 1823, he had proclaimed, "I believe it the best school in the world."

But by the time he became president, Jackson seems to have experienced a change of heart. He certainly made Thayer's life more difficult by reversing sixteen of the superintendent's dismissal orders in his first two years alone. Thayer indignantly protested that Jackson "is in the habit of dispensing with the most important regulations of the Academy in favor of his friends." It soon became clear to cadets who ran afoul of Thayer's regulations that an appeal to the White House would almost invariably bring about a restoration to duty.

Jackson's reelection in 1832 convinced Thayer that a showdown with the president was inevitable. He dispatched Captain Ethan Allen Hitchcock, his commandant of cadets, to Washington for an audience with Jackson in order to clear the air. Concurrently, he wrote to Secretary of War Lewis Cass, "I am led to believe that there is something at this institution which does not altogether meet with the president's approbation, but I am at a loss to conjecture whether the dissatisfaction, if such really exists, relates to persons or things." Although Cass replied that the president bore "not the slightest shade of unkindly feeling toward you," the tone of Jackson's meeting with Hitchcock indicated otherwise. "Sylvanus Thayer is a tyrant!" he shouted at the young captain. "The autocrat of all the Russias couldn't exercise more power."

Disconsolate, Thayer decided that his continued presence at West Point would only risk bringing the president's wrath down on the institution as a whole. On January 19, 1833, he wrote out a brief letter: "I have the honor to tender my resignation as superintendent of the military academy and to request that I may be relieved with as little delay as practicable." The War Department accepted it without comment. Thayer remained at West Point until the completion of final examinations that June. After the commencement service and the noisy celebration were over, every member of the graduating class called on the superintendent one by one to offer a handshake and a private word of farewell and, perhaps, of thanks.

> " THIS COURSE MAY IN THE END OCCASION MY REMOVAL, BUT IN THE MEANTIME I SHALL HAVE DONE SOME GOOD AND PERFORMED MY DUTY."
>
> — SUPERINTENDENT SYLVANUS THAYER

Medals of Academic Merit circa 1866

Thayer had insisted that no formal ceremony attend his departure, and did not even announce the date. On the warm, pleasant evening of July 1, he walked alone down the steep path that led from the grassy Plain to the dock on the river. There he found a knot of officers gathered to wait for arrival of the New York–bound steamboat. They conversed casually as the boat tied up to the quay and unloaded cargo and a handful of passengers. Then, as the crew prepared to cast off the lines, Thayer turned to the small

group and, to their collective astonishment, abruptly announced "Good-bye, gentlemen." He stepped aboard the boat and was gone.

A comment Thayer himself made some years earlier may serve as the best epitaph for his steadfast commitment to upholding excellence at his beloved Academy: "This course may in the end occasion my removal, but in the mean-time I shall have done some good and performed my duty."

The Thayer Era did not end with the superintendent's muted send-off. His tenure was sufficiently long that, by 1833, every professor at the Academy had been appointed by Thayer—and most of them were alumni. They continued his policies and maintained his curriculum to such a degree that cadets who graduated years after Thayer left West Point could be said to be products of his system.

In the decade following Thayer's departure, the United States faced no external threats to its security. The problems with Native Americans along the frontier presented a continuing but low-intensity conflict. The regular army remained at its peacetime levels, and chances for advancement within the officer corps were slim. Lieutenants often waited twenty-five years for their company commanders to retire in order to receive their captain's bars. For this reason, in 1835 and 1836 alone almost 120 officers resigned their commissions.

Under these circumstances, the greatest opportunities for West Pointers, with their invaluable engineering degrees, lay in the civilian rather than the military sector. The Academy's Board of Visitors said as much in one of its periodic reports: "It should be universally known through the Nation that the object of the instruction which is given at the Military School at West Point, is, not only to prepare young men to fill the vacancies which occur in the Corps of Engineers, Artillery, and Infantry of the Army, but also to prepare them to occupy other useful stations in the service of the General Government." In other words, a recent graduate could render far greater benefit as chief engineer for one of the nation's burgeoning railroad lines or canal companies than by languishing as a second lieutenant in some moldering coastal fortification. Cadet James

Above: *Robert W. Weir was head of the West Point Department of Drawing from 1834 to 1876.*

USMA Archives

Left: The Snow Plow *(1872) was painted during Weir's USMA tenure. During this time Weir established himself as a prominent American painter of the century.*

West Point Museum Collections, USMA

Opposite: *Sylvanus Thayer served the longest tenure as super-intendent in Academy history. This monument was erected in 1883.*

© Robert Stewart

Burbridge commented: "I am well aware that engineering at this time is one of the most lucrative & honorable proffessions [*sic*] that a young man can get in to."

America's infrastructure experienced a staggering building boom during this period, as new transportation arteries spread up and down the East Coast and across the Appalachian Mountains into the interior—and almost every project was planned and executed by a West Point–trained engineer. "These are some of the enduring memorials of the usefulness of the Military Academy," declared a congressional committee, "and of the returns it has made for the care, and time, and money which have been bestowed upon it."

Cadets test model bridges in engineering lab. Engineering graduates of the Military Academy were much in demand in the private sector to help build the nation's infrastructure.
USMA Archives

But this situation changed drastically in 1846 when, for the first time in more than a quarter century, the United States found itself at war with a foreign power. Here, finally, was the opportunity for West Pointers to put their military skills to use in the country's service—and not inconsequentially, to gain promotions as well. Cadet George B. McClellan, a distinguished student who ranked second in the Class of 1846, reveled at the news that the country had declared war on Mexico. "War at last sure enough! Ain't it glorious! 15,000 regulars and 50,000 volunteers!"

The senior American generals in the Mexican War, Zachary Taylor and Winfield Scott, had received their commissions directly from civilian life, but the field-grade officers of their armies—the regimental and battalion commanders, the engineers and artillerists—were graduates of Sylvanus Thayer's Military Academy. No doubt, the former superintendent took great pride in the excellent service they rendered, which stood in stark contrast to West Pointers' meager contributions during the War of 1812. A total of 523 graduates took part in the war, and no fewer than 452 received brevet promotions as a mark of their performance. The U.S. Army did not have a system at that time for recognizing gallantry by awarding medals, but higher rank—and the commensurate pay—probably meant more to them in any case.

The nearby Hudson provided opportunities for training in pontoon bridge construction.

General Scott stated unequivocally, "I give it as my fixed opinion, that but for our graduated cadets, the war between the United States and Mexico might, and probably would, have lasted some four or five years, with, in its first half, more defeats than victories falling to our share; whereas in less than two campaigns, we conquered a great country and a peace, without the loss of a single battle or skirmish."

The list of Academy graduates who distinguished themselves in the Mexican War—Lee, Grant, Jackson, Sherman, Longstreet, Sheridan, Hill, Meade, Beauregard, Hooker—reads like a register of American military history. They had forged bonds of friendship during the summer encampments, in the classrooms, and on the drill fields of West Point. Their baptism of fire at Veracruz, Monterrey, Buena Vista, and Chapultepec had strengthened that sense of closeness and truly made them a "band of brothers."

When the war ended in 1848 with a resounding American triumph, these officers, these comrades went back to peacetime duty or returned to civilian life. None would have dared suspect that more than a decade later, they would find themselves caught up in a much larger conflict, a terrible war that would pit classmate against classmate, friend against friend, brother against brother.

General Winfield Scott was greatly impressed by the performance of West Point graduates in the Mexican War.

CHAPTER FOUR

1848—1865

A HOUSE DIVIDED

"By his generous, manly and consistent conduct he has won the respect and esteem of every Cadet in the Corps." Thus did one student at the U.S. Military Academy describe Brevet Colonel Robert E. Lee, who had returned to his alma mater on September 1, 1852, to assume the superintendency of the institution he had attended under the tutelage of Sylvanus Thayer. Lee had graduated second in the Class of 1829 with an exemplary academic record. But even more remarkable was the fact that his four-year term at West Point was unblemished by so much as a single demerit for disciplinary infractions. He was one of the few cadets to accomplish this notable feat.

Scion of a distinguished Virginia family—his father was Revolutionary War hero Henry "Light-Horse Harry" Lee—young Robert seemed destined from childhood for a military career. One of his secondary school teachers in Alexandria, Virginia, characterized Lee as "a most exemplary student in every respect. He was never behind time at his

Academy graduates served as commanders on both sides of the Civil War. Ranald S. Mackenzie, shown here in 1862 (seated at left), rose to the rank of brevet major general in the Union army.

© CORBIS

studies; never failed in a single recitation; was perfectly observant of the rules and regulations of the institution; was gentlemanly, unobtrusive, and respectful."

Many years later an officer on Lee's staff wrote that he was "at once greatly attracted and greatly impressed by his appearance. [He had] strikingly handsome features, bright and penetrating eyes, his iron-gray hair closely cut, his face cleanly shaved except a mustache, he appeared every inch a soldier and a man born to command."

When Lee graduated from West Point, his high standing earned him a commission in the prestigious Corps of Engineers. Unlike many of his fellow graduates who resigned during the 1830s to pursue lucrative careers in private industry, Lee remained with the army during these lean years, designing and building a variety of fortifications along the East Coast.

By all accounts, Mary Randolph Custis Lee enjoyed her time at West Point while her husband, Robert E. Lee, was superintendent.

Library of Congress

Still, his frustration sometimes showed; it had taken him seven years, for example, to advance from second to first lieutenant. Writing to a friend who had opted for the life of a civilian engineer, Lee complained, "You ask what are my prospects in the Corps? Bad enough—unless it is increased and something is done for us."

During this period his life did take one positive turn that would have a lasting impact. He made the acquaintance of Mary Randolph Custis, a distant relative of George Washington, whose stately family estate, Arlington, was situated on the heights across the Potomac River from the nation's capital. After a suitable interlude of genteel courtship, Lee proposed and Mary accepted. The couple were married in the mansion's front parlor on June 30, 1831.

Whenever possible, Mary accompanied her husband to his various army postings. But that proved impossible when war with Mexico came in 1846, and Lee—finally promoted to captain—was assigned to the staff of General Winfield Scott, whose army was advancing on Mexico City. Soon after his arrival at Scott's headquarters, Lee's career—and his life—was almost cut short by a case of mistaken identity. Another member of Scott's staff recounted the incident: "Capt. R. E. Lee, one of the engineers, and an admirable officer, had a narrow escape with his life yesterday. Returning from a working party with Lieut. P. G. T. Beauregard, he turned a point in the path in the bushes, and suddenly came upon one of our soldiers who no doubt mistook him for a Mexican and challenged 'Who comes there?' 'Friends!' said Captain Lee. 'Officers' said Beauregard at the same time, but the soldier, in trepidation and haste, levelled [sic] a pistol at Lee and fired. The ball passed between his left arm and body,—the flame singeing his coat, he was so near."

Despite the narrow escape, the dashing young officer went on to prove his mettle on the battlefield as ably as he had in the realm of peacetime engineering. Lee won this unstinting accolade from General Scott himself: "I am compelled to make special mention of the services of Captain R. E. Lee, Engineer. This officer, greatly distinguished at the siege

of Vera Cruz, was again indefatigable, during these operations, in reconnaisances as daring as laborious, and of the utmost value. Nor was he less conspicuous in planting [artillery] batteries, and in conducting columns to their stations under heavy fire from the enemy." By war's end Captain Lee had earned the universal respect of all officers who served with him—Scott called him "the very best soldier I ever saw in the field." For his wartime service, he earned three brevet promotions in 1847.

Many of Lee's fellow West Pointers who had returned to army service to fight in Mexico resumed their civilian careers after the cessation of hostilities. Lee, on the other hand, once again took up the more mundane life of a peacetime fortifications engineer. But his war record had not been forgotten, and in September 1852 he received the assignment of superintendent of the Military Academy. The transfer pleased him and Mary greatly since it allowed the Lee family, which now included seven children, to finally settle into a conventional domestic life. The assignment was made all the sweeter by the fact that Lee's eldest son, George Washington Custis Lee, and his nephew Fitzhugh Lee were both cadets at this time.

This view of "Professors' Row" demonstrates the idyllic scenery of West Point when Lee served as superintendent.
USMA Archives

Appointed superintendent in 1838, Major Richard Delafield, Class of 1818, was responsible for the design and construction of many new buildings at West Point.

The U.S. Military Academy had just celebrated its fiftieth anniversary when Robert E. Lee became superintendent. Having proven itself as a steadfast supplier of well-trained professional soldiers to serve America in war as well as a provider of skilled engineers to meet the country's peacetime needs, West Point had withstood numerous challenges to its function, direction, management—even its very existence—over the past five decades. By the middle of the nineteenth century, the school had become firmly established in the consciousness of both the American public and the country's political leadership as a cherished national institution.

The Corps of Cadets was roughly the same size—about two hundred in all—as it had been when Lee was a plebe. But in physical appearance the Military Academy to which he returned had changed dramatically. One of Lee's predecessors in the post of superintendent, Major Richard Delafield, who had graduated at the top of the Class of 1818, had undertaken an ambitious expansion program during the late 1830s and 1840s. Delafield had overseen the construction of a new chapel, hospital, barracks, mess hall, classroom building, library, riding hall, and stables. Delafield's penchant for the Tudor-Gothic architectural style gave West Point the distinctive countenance it bears to this day. Clad in slate-gray granite and sporting such Gothic features as turrets, serrated rooflines, and sally ports, the new buildings were, in Delafield's opinion, "not only pleasing to the eye, but suited to the scenery." One cadet of this period remarked that the Academy was beginning to resemble a "great stone castle."

The Old Cadet Chapel built in 1836 was the first house of worship at the Academy.

In other respects West Point had changed little since the days of Sylvanus Thayer. The curriculum still retained his emphasis on mathematics as the foundation of an engineering degree, much to the frustration of many cadets. In a letter to his father, Cadet Edward Hartz noted that "in the history of the Institution no one has ever stood head [of his class] but he who has an extraordinary talent for Mathematics." But Cadet James Ewing expressed the sentiments of countless fellow sufferers when he wrote on the flyleaf of his calculus text, "God damn all mathematics to the lowest depths of hell!!" And Cadet George Cushing explained to his father that "I can't write as good a letter as I used to—as I am always thinking of Math.—I have a nightmare every night almost of it. —Gigantic X's

and Y's, +'s and −'s squat on me—and amuse themselves in sticking me with equations, and pounding me on the head."

The chair of the department, Professor Albert Church, who had been at the Academy since Thayer's day, was likened by one cadet to "an old mathematical cinder, bereft of all natural feeling." Another cadet penned a whimsical ode to the travails of Church's course: "Of all the girls I ever knew, / The one I've most neglected, / Is Called Miss 'Anna Lytical,' / For her I've least respected. / Oh! Anna! Anna Lytical / I'll never love you more / For you, I fear, will cause my fall, / And make me leave the Corps."

As superintendent, Lee did oversee one sweeping yet short-lived modification to the curriculum. The Academy's Board of Visitors had long maintained that cadets would benefit from classes in the humanities as well as increased practical training in the military sciences. In 1854 Secretary of War Jefferson Davis expanded the course of study from four

The Dean's House, located on "Professors' Row," is a classic Hudson River Valley Victorian villa, built around 1857.

© Ted Spiegel

A cavalry cadet troop readies for inspection on the Plain (circa 1903). Cavalry training at the Military Academy began in 1839 and continued through World War II.

USMA Archives

years to five, with additional classes in Spanish, history, geography, and military jurisprudence. The change proved unpopular with professors and students alike, and would last less than a decade.

Major Delafield's construction of horse stables and a riding hall had allowed the addition of a field of study that was much more amenable to the cadets—equestrian training. One cadet in particular from rural Ohio, whose student career was otherwise undistinguished, gained widespread acclaim for his enthralling proficiency on horseback. Ulysses S. Grant attended West Point in the early 1840s and, therefore, was not present during Robert E. Lee's tenure as superintendent, but their paths would cross—with momentous consequences—in the years to come.

In many ways Grant, a product of modest, midwestern circumstances, represented the antithesis of Lee. As a youth he had expressed no desire to attend West Point. When Ulysses' father informed him that he had arranged a congressional appointment, the son

replied, "But I won't go. [My father] said he thought I would, *and I thought so too, if he did.*"
The young Grant "had a very exalted idea of the aquirements necessary to get through
[the Academy]. I did not believe I possessed them, and could not bear the idea of failing."

Still, Grant agreed to go, in part because, "I had always a great desire to travel [and
going] to West Point would give me the opportunity of visiting the two great cities of the
continent, Philadelphia and New York. This was enough. When these places were visited I
would have been glad to have had a steamboat or railroad collision, or any
other accident happen, by which I might have received a temporary injury
sufficient to make me ineligible, for a time, to enter the Academy. Nothing
of the kind occurred, and I had to face the music."

The prospective cadet enjoyed a leisurely journey up the Ohio

USMA Archives

" A MILITARY LIFE HAD NO CHARMS FOR ME, AND I HAD NOT THE FAINTEST IDEA OF STAYING IN THE ARMY EVEN IF I SHOULD BE GRADUATED, WHICH I DID NOT EXPECT."

— U L Y S S E S   S .   G R A N T

River and across the Alleghenies in the spring of 1839, "and got
reprimanded from home afterwards, for dallying by the way so long. I
reported at West Point on the 30th or 31st of May, and about two weeks
later passed my examination for admission, without difficulty, very
much to my surprise."

Grant was one of those middle-of-the-pack cadets who held no
illusions about receiving an engineer's commission at the end of four years.
Nor did the prospect of an officer's career hold any great appeal. "A military
life had no charms for me," he candidly admitted in his memoirs, written late in his life, "and I
had not the faintest idea of staying in the army even if I should be graduated, which I did not
expect." Consequently, he was, at best, an indifferent student. "I did not take hold of my
studies with avidity, in fact I rarely ever read over a lesson the second time during my entire
cadetship. I could not sit in my room doing nothing. There is a fine library connected with
the Academy from which the cadets can get books to read in their quarters. I devoted more
time to these, than to books relating to the course of studies. Much of the time, I am sorry to
say, was devoted to novels, but not those of the trashy sort." Unlike so many of his fellow
cadets, Professor Church's class held no special terrors for him. "Mathematics was very easy

*This Daguerrotype
shows a 21-year-old
Ulysses S. Grant
(Class of 1843)
in Louisiana in 1845.*

West Point's equestrian team competes around the country. Historically, Generals Ulysses Grant and George Patton were among the more proficient of the Academy's horsemen.

© Ted Spiegel

to me," Grant remarked, "so that when January came, I passed the examination, taking a good standing in that branch."

The one area of West Point's curriculum in which Ulysses Grant truly excelled was horsemanship. "It was as good as any circus to see Grant ride," one of his classmates noted enthusiastically, and many cadets slipped away from other duties to go to the riding hall just to watch him perform. Even as a young child, "horses seemed to understand him," his mother recalled. Still, on one occasion Cadet Grant was written up by the riding instructor for "cruel and inhumane treatment of a dumb animal, i.e., he kicked his horse." In his own defense, Grant simply responded, "The horse kicked me first."

Grant's finest moment came one day in the riding hall astride a tall, strong-willed, chestnut-colored mount named York, who had a fearsome reputation for throwing off mediocre riders then performing the rest of the exercise alone and without mistake. But York had taken a fancy to Grant, and on this occasion, before the assembled Board of Visitors and a large throng of spectators, the riding instructor called upon them to execute a special drill. He had an orderly hold a long pole at arm's length over his head with the other end braced against the building's wall. Then, at the given signal, Grant and York took a running start and soared over the pole, "coming down with a tremendous thud" amid tumultuous applause. At the crowd's urging, horse and rider executed three encores, clearing the barrier with ease each time.

Cadet Grant graduated in 1843 and received a second lieutenant's commission in the infantry. He performed solidly if unspectacularly as a regimental quartermaster and brevet captain with Winfield Scott's army in Mexico, demonstrating personal bravery and coolness under enemy fire. One day Grant reported to Scott's headquarters with his clothing somewhat dusty and disheveled from the demands of his job. There he was politely but firmly upbraided by a handsome, immaculately dressed member of the general's staff. "I feel it my duty, Captain, to call your attention to General Scott's order that an officer reporting to headquarters should be in full uniform," Robert E. Lee pointed out.

After the war—and despite his earlier protestations—Grant remained in the officer corps, serving at various posts in the Far West and eventually rising to the regular army rank of captain. But by 1854 financial concerns caused him to reconsider. "My family, all this while, was in the east," he wrote. "It consisted now of a wife and two children. I saw no chance of supporting them on the Pacific coast out of my pay as an army officer. I concluded, therefore, to resign. . . ." He looked back with mostly fond memories of his army career and regaled his friends and family for years with stories of his experiences in

Mexico—the beauty of the country and the terrible cost of the war. And he often recounted that one, brief incident with the dashing staff officer at army headquarters, little knowing that the two would meet again in years to come under far different circumstances.

Above: While at the Academy, Grant completed several sketches and drawings that still survive today. Below: Ranked twenty-first in a class of thirty-nine cadets, Grant was an ambivalent cadet. During 1839 and 1840 his list of delinquencies included "sitting down on post" and "late at artillery drill roll call."

© Ted Spiegel

At West Point, Superintendent Robert E. Lee was still administering discipline in the same compassionate manner he had demonstrated in dealing with the scruffy young officer in Mexico. It simply was not within the man's nature to mete out punishment with an iron fist as many of his predecessors had done. Once while out riding he came across three cadets who were enjoying an unauthorized outing far from the Academy grounds. Catching sight of the superintendent, the three hopped over a fence and disappeared into the woods. With an air of resignation, Lee remarked, "I wish boys would do what is right. It would be so much easier for all parties."

On another occasion two cadets, Archibald Gracie Jr. and Wharton Green, got into a fight on the parade ground. One of the tactical officers collared Gracie, but Green escaped unnoticed. When ordered by the instructor to name his antagonist, Gracie replied, "You will have to ask him, for I'm no informer." He was immediately placed under arrest. The next day Green presented himself at Lee's office. "Mr. Gracie was yesterday reported for fighting on the parade ground," he said, "and the 'other fellow' was not." "Yes, sir," replied Lee, "and I presume you are 'the other fellow.'" Green confessed, and added, "Whatever punishment is meted out to him, I insist on having the same given to me."

"The offense," Lee cautioned the cadet, "entails a heavy penalty." But Green remained steadfast: "I am aware of the fact, Colonel, but Mr. Gracie is not entitled to a monopoly of it." Then, perhaps moved by Cadet Green's forthrightness, Superintendent Lee decided to overlook the incident and let them both off. "Don't you think," he added, "that it is better for brothers to dwell together in peace and harmony?" Chastened but wiser for the experience, Green replied, "Yes, Colonel, and if we were all like you, it would be an easy thing to do."

Above: *Walking a post for a determined number of hours is one form of discipline common to cadets at West Point.*
© Robert Stewart

Opposite: *Grant's portrait keeps a watchful eye over cadets studying in the library.*
© Bob Krist

As a rule, Lee was more inclined to encourage good conduct than to punish bad. Reflecting on the example of civility and integrity set by the superintendent himself, Cadet John Bell Hood recalled, "His uniform kindness to me whilst I was a cadet, inclined me the more willingly to receive and remember this fatherly advice; and from these early relations first sprang my affection and veneration which grew in strength to the end of his career." Lee frequently wrote to the families of cadets who were facing dismissal for disciplinary infractions, hoping that parental support might help foster a change in attitude and behavior.

His own nephew Fitzhugh, an exuberant young man who was universally well liked within the Corps of Cadets, spent his entire four years on the verge of dismissal for excessive demerits. Though Lee would never have shown his nephew any favoritism, by the same token he would not have hesitated to offer the wayward lad the same encouragement and counsel he bestowed on the rest of his charges, which is probably the reason that Fitzhugh managed to graduate—albeit fifth from the bottom of his class—in 1856.

Parents often wrote to Lee requesting that their sons be excused from class to come home for certain important family functions. Rather than rejecting such applications

Above: *As superin-tendent, Lee approved a new design for the cadet shako.*
USMA Archives

Below right: *This 1853 drawing shows Lee's sig-nature and verification of the existing cap design before the changes.*
Below left: *The cadet dress cap today.*

© Ted Spiegel

Present Cadet dress cap.
Black felt, patent leather top.
weight. 10¾ oz.   cost $2.00

Engineer Dept – April 4. 1853
Received with Col. R. E. Lee's letter dated
April 1. 1853 –(Mil Acad 399)

West Point Museum Collections, USMA

A TALENTED MISFIT

*I*n modern parlance Cadet James McNeill Whistler would be called a class clown. Whistler, who arrived at West Point in 1851, demonstrated an obvious artistic genius in drawing class, but he bedeviled instructors in other courses with his nonchalant, almost seditious attitude. Once, during a history lesson on the Mexican War, he freely admitted his ignorance of the subject. "What!" the professor exclaimed, "you do not know the date of the battle of Buena Vista? Suppose you were to go out to dinner and the company began to talk of the Mexican War, and you, a West Point man, were asked the date of the battle. What would you do?" To which Whistler serenely replied, "Do? Why, I should refuse to associate with people who could talk of such things at dinner."

The young cadet, affectionately known as Curly by his classmates, also demonstrated an almost abnormal lack of aptitude in the riding hall. During one exercise his mount stopped short, causing him to pitch forward out of the saddle and land on the floor. "Mr. Whistler," the riding instructor called out, "I am pleased to see you for once at the head of your class."

Whistler's sardonic nature even surfaced in his favorite course. Professor Weir, the drawing instructor, had a habit of touching up what he considered deficiencies in his students' artwork. One day as he approached Whistler's easel, pen in hand, the cadet raised his arms and cried out in mock indignation, "Oh, don't sir, don't! You'll spoil it!" On another occasion Weir assigned him to produce an engineer's rendering of a bridge. Whistler sketched the structure, then impulsively added two young boys lounging on its deck. Reproached by the instructor, he redrew the bridge, moving the boys to the riverbank below. Weir's patience ran thin as he ordered the cadet to eliminate the figures entirely. Obstinate to the end, Whistler's third effort included two small tombstones beside the stream.

The last straw came during a chemistry course that Whistler attended as a Second Classman. When the instructor called on him to discuss the properties of silicon, he audaciously tried to bluff his way through. "I am required to discuss the subject of silicon," he began. "Silicon is a gas . . ." At which point the instructor broke in, "That will do, Mr. Whistler." Soon thereafter, he was dismissed for academic deficiency. Even the usually lenient Superintendent Robert E. Lee refused his appeal for reinstatement. Later in life, after he had achieved widespread fame as an artist, Whistler recounted the incident to friends with typical drollness: "Had silicon been a gas, I would have been a major general."

Above: One of the best-known cadets who never graduated, James Whistler entered the Academy in 1851, did not do well in his studies, and left in 1854. Below and bottom: Four sketches by Whistler humorously depict each half hour of a cadet shift on post.

Last half hour!

with a peremptory note—as one can imagine Thayer doing—Lee took the time to respond at length. To one such request in February 1853, he replied to a father, "I regret that I cannot with propriety grant the leave of absence to your son you desire to attend a wedding in your family on the 17th. I have been obliged to refuse many similar applications; for what is granted to one must be given to all; & you can readily see the serious interruptions that would take place to their studies and duties. The whole time of the Cadets is necessary to master their Course at the Academy, & any withdrawal of their attention affects them injuriously."

Lee made a practice of inviting the Corps of Cadets, few at a time, to his quarters, where he and Mary would put on small but elegant soirees. Their young daughter Agnes recorded in her diary, "We have had so many [dinner parties] . . . that the whole family are heartily sick of them. We declare that they are Pa's delight but he maintains he dislikes them very much." The cadets, grateful for any break in their numbing daily routine, enjoyed the affairs, and were especially impressed on those occasions when the Lees would break out the silverware that Mary had inherited from George Washington.

Lee also took time from his busy schedule to write a letter of recommendation for a former cadet and fellow Mexican War veteran: "Understanding that Major Thomas J. Jackson late of the U.S. Army is a candidate for the vacant chair of mathematics in the University of Virginia, I take pleasure in bearing testimony to his character and his merit."

Thomas Jackson had been an even more unlikely candidate for success at West Point than Ulysses Grant. Reared in the backwoods of western Virginia, he had acquired only a rudimentary primary education. According to a classmate, Jackson "could add up a column of figures, but as to vulgar or decimal fractions, it is doubtful if he had ever heard of them." No one present at his entrance examination ever forgot the spectacle of the large, obviously ill-at-ease man dressed in simple homespun garments as he shambled to the front of the room to face the faculty. "His whole soul was bent upon passing," another cadet recalled.

USMA Archives

" IT GRIEVES ME TO THINK THAT IN A SHORT TIME I MUST BE SEPARATED FROM AMIABLE & MERITORIOUS FRIENDS WHOM AN ACQUAINTANCE OF YEARS HAS ENDEARED TO ME BY MANY TIES."

— T H O M A S   " S T O N E W A L L "   J A C K S O N

Thomas J. "Stonewall" Jackson, Class of 1846, was among a group of cadets that comprised one of West Point's most illustrious classes.

"When he went to the blackboard the perspiration was streaming from his face, and during the whole examination his anxiety was painful to witness. While trying to work out his example in fractions, the cuffs of his coat, first the right and then the left, were brought into requisition to wipe off the perspiration." As he returned to his seat, "every member of the examining board turned away his head to hide the smile which could not be suppressed."

When the board posted its list of applicants found "duly qualified," the very last name at the bottom of the sheet was Tom Jackson. He validated the board's faith by working harder than any cadet in memory, regularly staying up past lights-out to study by the glow of his coal grate. With piercing blue-gray eyes that seemed to look right through a man and a dour countenance that discouraged others from engaging him in good-natured small talk, Jackson did not win many friends among the Corps of Cadets. Yet his single-minded focus made a lasting impression on his classmates. "No one I have ever known," one recalled, "could so perfectly withdraw his mind from surrounding objects or influences, and so thoroughly involve his whole being in the subject under consideration."

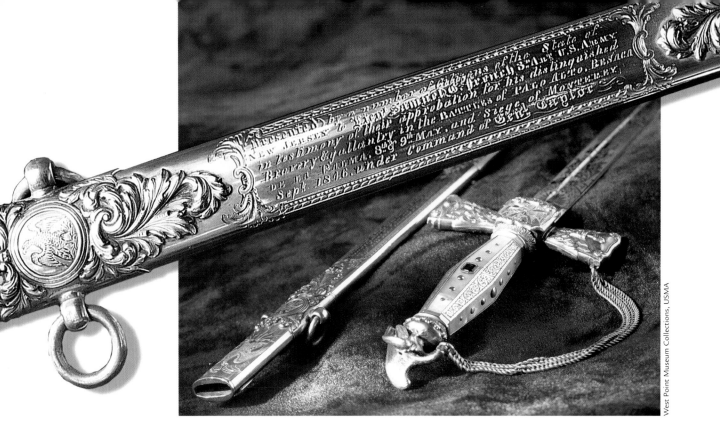

Like many of his fellow West Pointers, Samuel G. French served admirably in the Mexican War. This sword and scabbard were presented to French by the citizens of New Jersey in recognition of his bravery during the war.

Cadet Dabney Maury observed, "Cold and undemonstrative as he was, he was absolutely honest and kindly, intensely attending to his own business." Cadet Parmenas Taylor Turnley added, "While there were many who seemed to surpass him in intellect, in geniality, and in good-fellowship, there was no one of our class who more absolutely possessed the respect and confidence of all." And First Classman Ulysses Grant said of the plebe who, like himself, sprang from humble roots that seemed to belie his prospects at such an imposing institution, "He had so much courage and energy, worked so hard, and governed his life by a discipline so stern."

Jackson himself seems to have regarded his fellow cadets with more affection than he was capable of showing them. "It grieves me," he disclosed in a letter to his sister, "to think that in a short time I must be separated from amiable & meritorious friends whom an acquaintance of years has endeared to me by many ties." Over the span of four years, Jackson steadily improved his academic standing, and eventually ranked seventeenth out of fifty-nine in the Class of 1846—the largest in West Point's history up to that time. A fellow graduate noted that "if we stay here another year, old Jack will be head of the class."

Assigned to the artillery corps, Jackson served admirably in the Mexican War, earning permanent promotion to first lieutenant and two brevet promotions to major. Afterward, he left the army and landed a professorship at the Virginia Military Institute teaching natural and experimental philosophy and, not surprisingly, artillery tactics. Jackson, like Grant, might have spent the rest of his life in relative obscurity as just another former army officer and Mexican War veteran, but for an issue that, by the 1850s, was already beginning to tear the country apart.

The institution of slavery in the southern states polarized America, creating splits within political parties and society as a whole. Yet the bonds forged by their shared experiences at West Point enabled cadets from both North and South to ignore—at least at first—the sectionalism that had begun to affect the rest of the country. Cadet Oliver O. Howard, a staunch abolitionist, became close friends with Cadet James Ewell Brown Stuart, a slaveholder from Virginia. Even though Stuart's position was diametrically opposed to Howard's, he nonetheless wrote in 1851 that "there seems to be a sentiment of mutual forbearance" within the Corps of Cadets. Another cadet reported to his father that the national debate "does not lead to any open rupture but rather tends to draw out our individual sympathy for each other."

Many northern cadets did not share Howard's views on slavery in any case. One cadet from New York wrote, "Slavery may be a curse, but I cannot help thinking that anti-Slavery is a greater one." And Cadet George Armstrong Custer decried the "black-brown Republicans who will either deprive a portion of their fellow citizens of their just rights or produce a dissolution of the Union."

In the midst of this turbulent period, Robert E. Lee took his leave of West Point. He did so after less than three years as superintendent as the only means available to obtain promotion within the small peacetime army. Despite his brevet promotions and his stellar

Union officer George Armstrong Custer, Class of 1861, poses with a captured Confederate officer, James B. Washington, Class of 1863. There were strong personal bonds between West Pointers who fought on both sides of the Civil War.

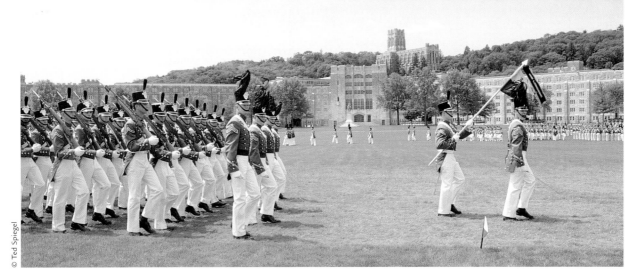

Cadet parades on the Plain are an impressive sight. Thousands of visitors come to West Point each year to watch the cadets pass in full dress review.

record during twenty-six years of service, Lee still held the regular rank of captain in the Corps of Engineers in 1855, with no prospects of advancement in sight. A transfer to the cavalry, which was actively engaged on the frontier in a running war with Native Americans, offered him the chance for immediate promotion to major.

Lee's family, which had made a comfortable life at West Point and enjoyed the company of the Corps of Cadets, was dismayed by the move. Daughter Agnes noted in her diary, "But second thoughts—Papa's going way out West, and—and leaving West Point, that I now almost consider as home, was very sad. We all regret it now." On a spring weekend in May 1855, as the family prepared to

> **" BUT SECOND THOUGHTS—PAPA'S GOING WAY OUT WEST, AND—AND LEAVING WEST POINT, THAT I NOW ALMOST CONSIDER AS HOME, WAS VERY SAD. WE ALL REGRET IT NOW. "**
>
> — A G N E S   L E E

leave, she added, "I looked out on parade that evening for the *last* time. How strangely it sounded as I repeated to myself 'my last parade.' I couldn't realize it."

The cadets gave the Lees a warm and heartfelt send-off, gathering outside the superintendent's quarters to serenade them with "Home Sweet Home" and "Carry Me Back to Old Virginny." The next morning the boat dock on the Hudson below the parade ground was crowded with those wishing to "bid a last, a long farewell." Agnes concluded the final entry in her diary on her family's life at West Point by noting that "the Heavens seemed to sympathize with us, it shed torrents of tears & as we crossed the river in open boats everything was pretty well soaked."

At the Military Academy the mood of "mutual forbearance" that Cadet Jeb Stuart had described continued more or less intact until October 1859, when a firebrand named John Brown led a small party of fellow abolitionists on a raid against the U.S. arsenal at Harpers

Ferry, Virginia. Hoping to inspire a slave revolt, Brown and his men were instead surrounded and captured by a hastily gathered detachment of federal troops under the command of a cavalry officer on temporary leave from his western regiment. On orders from the War Department, Robert E. Lee had rushed from the family home at Arlington to quell the uprising.

When news of the abortive raid reached West Point, it caused an uproar and hardened positions on both sides of the slavery debate, driving a deep wedge between northern and southern cadets. Arguments became frequent; occasional fights broke out. One particularly serious brawl erupted between Cadet Wade Hampton Gibbes of South Carolina and Cadet Emory Upton of Pennsylvania. Upton, an avowed abolitionist, had attended liberal Oberlin College in Ohio, one of the few institutions of that time to admit black students and women. In the heated atmosphere following John Brown's raid, Gibbes was heard to accuse Upton of having had liaisons with African American females at the school. Upton promptly challenged him to a fight, which took place one evening after dinner in a barracks room packed with supporters of both adversaries. Gibbes and Upton went at each other tooth and nail, bloodying faces and blackening eyes until one of Gibbes's southern friends called out for him to use his bayonet, at which point everyone seemed to have realized that the situation was getting out of control. The fight stopped and the cadets dispersed; the authorities apparently never learned of the affair, for no disciplinary action was taken.

Guard mount at summer camp in the late 1800s.
USMA Archives

View of the Hudson River Valley from West Point in the mid-nineteenth century.
USMA Archives

As the election of 1860 drew nearer, the antagonism between North and South that would soon split the nation in two was mirrored at West Point. "Representing . . . as we did, every Congressional district," Cadet Morris Schaff observed sagely, "we were in miniature the country itself." He also noted that "a state of recklessness as to discipline and a new indifference to class standing, were more or less noticeable in the conduct of the entire corps."

" REPRESENTING . . . AS WE DID, EVERY CONGRESSIONAL DISTRICT, WE WERE IN MINIATURE THE COUNTRY ITSELF. "

— CADET MORRIS SCHAFF

A straw poll held in October 1860, one month before the election, caused more problems.

Schaff wrote that it was as if "some evil spirit stole his way into West Point and thence into the room of a couple of bitterly partisan Southerners in my division. The next day. . . a box was set up at a suitable place, with a request that cadets should deposit therein their preferences for President of the United States." Although Republican candidate Abraham Lincoln received a minority of the votes, the architects of the poll, who considered him inimical to their region's well-being, if not its very survival, tried to track down those cadets who had voted for him. As a result, more fights broke out.

Cadet Tully McCrea observed that the presidential election "has been the cause of much ill feeling among the cadets for the last few weeks. Nearly all take an active interest

Cadets pose for an 1860 photograph with one of the Academy's fire engines.

and are in favor of one or the other of the candidates." He added, "the southerners swore (as is customary with a great many of them), they threatened to do all kinds of terrible things and blustered around at a great rate. They were all going to resign, they said, if Lincoln was elected." Henry Dupont remarked that "There is an insane spirit here rampant on the secession question."

When Lincoln, in fact, won by a narrow margin, tensions reached a fever pitch. Within weeks a group of cadets from South Carolina had penned an incendiary letter to their home state's *Columbia Guardian:* "We cannot so stifle our convictions of duty as to serve under such a man as Mr. Lincoln as our commander-in-chief." In a letter to his mother, Cadet William Harris wrote, "I think it would pain you, as it has me, to witness the effect which this struggle has produced in the Army & especially in the Corps of Cadets. Some of my own class who are appointed from South Carolina have received positive orders from home to come there immediately in the case of Lincoln's election." Then Harris added sorrowfully, "It seems inevitable that we must lose some of the finest fellows in our class."

Harris's prediction was soon borne out: Cadet Henry S. Farley of South Carolina resigned from the Academy on November 19—one month before his state seceded from the Union. Many southern cadets wrote their elected representatives asking what they should do. Cadet Thomas Rowland noted that his governor "advises all cadets from Virginia to remain here and do their duty until their native state shall absolutely require their services." A letter from a family friend advised Cadet John Pelham "to

> **I THINK IT WOULD PAIN YOU, AS IT HAS ME, TO WITNESS THE EFFECT WHICH THIS STRUGGLE HAS PRODUCED IN THE ARMY & ESPECIALLY IN THE CORPS OF CADETS. IT SEEMS INEVITABLE THAT WE MUST LOSE SOME OF THE FINEST FELLOWS IN OUR CLASS.**
>
> — CADET WILLIAM HARRIS

resign immediately after Alabama secedes and tender your sword to her."

In the midst of this crisis, on January 23, 1861, Captain P. G. T. Beauregard from Louisiana—who had been standing next to Robert E. Lee on that near-tragic day in Mexico—was named superintendent. A cadet from his home state promptly asked him whether he should resign. "Watch me," Beauregard replied, "and when I jump, you jump. What's the use of jumping too soon?" Beauregard was relieved after serving a mere five days, giving him the distinction of holding the shortest term as superintendent in the history of the Academy.

Following South Carolina's lead, the rest of the Deep South seceded during the next two months. Native Virginians—from Cadet Thomas Rowland to Major Robert E. Lee—waited anxiously to see if their state would follow. "What is to become of our glorious Union?" Rowland wrote to his father. "Everyone seems to despair of its perpetuation, but I cannot give it up. I will catch at the last straw, and stand by the Union until all is hopelessly lost. Then we must cast our lot with Virginia and hope for the best."

At his inauguration in March 1861, Lincoln sounded a conciliatory note: "I have no purpose directly or indirectly to interfere with the institution of slavery in the States where it exists." But he also added an admonition that, "no State, upon its own mere action, can lawfully get out of the Union." At West Point, anxious cadets debated the speech "over and over again," as Schaff remembered, "sometimes long after 'taps' had sounded." Another cadet commented, "Mr. Lincoln's speeches are certainly among the poorest I have ever read. Most schoolboys could do better."

The crisis had, in any case, passed the point where mere words could salvage a

The candor expressed by the fiery Pierre Gustave Toutant Beauregard of Louisiana, Class of 1838, may have contributed to his being removed as superintendent after only five days.

reconciliation and avert civil war. The die was irrevocably cast when South Carolina state forces fired on the federal garrison manning Fort Sumter in Charleston Harbor on April 12, 1861. Lincoln's call for 75,000 volunteers in response to the assault stimulated the secession of four more states, including Virginia, making a total of eleven within the newly formed Confederate States of America. Cadet McCrea noted that "when the news of the firing on Fort Sumter was received the effect was instantaneous, every Northern cadet showed his true colors. . . . One could have heard us singing 'The Star Spangled Banner' in Cold Spring. It was the first time I ever saw the Southern contingent cowed. All of their northern allies had deserted them, and they were stunned."

By the end of April, sixty-five of the eighty-six cadets from southern states had left the Academy of their own accord or were dismissed for refusing to take an oath of allegiance to the United States. As the Corps of Cadets split apart to take opposite sides in what was sure to be a bloody conflict, fond farewells replaced the acrimonious debate over slavery and secession. Classmates and close friends were subdued by the realization that they might soon face each other on some distant battlefield. First Classman Pierce Young of Georgia wrote to his parents, "You and the others down there don't realize the sacrifice resigning means."

These two cannon at the entrance to the library commemorate the first and last shots of the Civil War.

On the day of his departure, Cadet Sergeant Charles Ball of Alabama stood up in the mess hall and called out, "Battalion attention! Good-bye, boys! God bless you all!" His classmates broke out in a cheer and carried Ball on their shoulders to the boat dock. The popular Fitzhugh Lee, who had returned to West Point to serve as an instructor, received a particularly warm send-off. Cadet McCrea noted, "it was a bitter day for him when he left, for he did not want to go and said that he hated to desert his old flag." Lee made the rounds in the barracks, shaking every cadet's hand, and, "with tears in his eyes . . . hoped, he said, that our recollections of him would be as happy as those he had of us."

Academy graduates from seceding states who were serving with the regular army faced the same heart-wrenching choice as their southern brethren in the Corps of Cadets. Many decided that loyalty to their homes, families, and neighbors superseded their allegiance to the United States, and resigned their commissions. Perhaps the most eloquent expression of the distress this decision engendered came from Robert E. Lee, who wrote to the commanding general of the army, Winfield Scott, on April 20, 1861:

Gen.,

Since my interview with you on the 18th inst., I have felt that I ought no longer retain my commission in the Army. I therefore tender my resignation, which I request you will recommend for acceptance. It would have been presented at once but for the struggle it has cost me to separate myself from a service to which I have devoted the best years of my life, and all the ability I possessed. During the whole of that time—more than a quarter of a century, I have experienced nothing but kindness from my superiors and a most cordial friendship from my comrades. To no one, General, have I been as much indebted as to yourself for uniform kindness and consideration, and it has always been my ardent

" SAVE IN DEFENSE OF MY NATIVE STATE, I NEVER DESIRE AGAIN TO DRAW MY SWORD."

— R O B E R T E . L E E

desire to merit your approbation. I shall carry to the grave the most grateful recollections of your kind consideration, and your name and fame shall always be dear to me. Save in defense of my native State, I never desire again to draw my sword. Be pleased to accept my most earnest wishes for the continuance of your happiness and prosperity, and believe me, most truly yours,

R. E. Lee

Grandson of "Light-Horse Harry" Lee and nephew of Robert E. Lee, Fitzhugh Lee, Class of 1856, was a popular cadet at the Military Academy.

USMA Archives

Above: *George Custer captured a baggage train with this coat belonging to Thomas Lafayette Rosser, a cadet who left the Academy in 1861 to join the South. Custer and Rosser were classmates and friends before the war and renewed their friendship again after it.* Below: *Grant's military successes during the Civil War brought him the rank of General of the Army, along with this distinctive uniform featuring three groups of buttons in double rows.*

West Point Museum Collections, USMA

At West Point, the cadets who remained had great difficulty focusing on their studies. Cadet McCrea observed that instructors "complain bitterly about the deficiency of cadets in their recitations and the Superintendent says that something will have to be done about it. I imagine the only way to prevent it is to stop the war, for it is impossible to confine the mind to dry abstractions in philosophy when our country is passing through the most trying ordeal since the Revolution."

The Class of 1861, on orders from the War Department, was graduated a month early and immediately sent to Washington to train and drill the volunteer units that were pouring into the capital. The Second Classmen then appealed for a similar dispensation in order to join the war effort, which was granted. They obtained their commissions in June, a full year ahead of schedule, leaving only ninety-eight cadets on the rolls of the Academy. No further classes would receive this special consideration, although the War Department did immediately abandon the five-year course of study.

As the Union war machine geared up, the cadets' instruction was hampered by the frequent turnover of army personnel at the Academy. In the next four years, three superintendents, six commandants of cadets, and numerous tactical officers and instructors would come and go. Artillery and cavalry training was suspended after all of West Point's guns and horses were transferred to the armies in the field. Meanwhile, the cadets yearned to join their recently graduated comrades. "I suppose there is a great deal of stir and preparation for war going on in the country," Cadet Cullen Bryant remarked in a letter to his father, "though I have as yet seen but very few evidences of it. We are almost completely secluded and shut out from the rest of the world." He went on to lament that "we might as well be at some frontier post a thousand miles from any settlement." Only through newspaper accounts could Bryant and his classmates follow the far-off cataclysmic events and the indelible exploits of the Academy's alumni.

The Civil War was a West Pointers' conflict from start to finish. Academy graduates commanded both sides in fifty-five of the war's sixty major

WEST POINT IN '63.

PHOTOGRAPHED AND PUBLISHED BY GEO. G. ROCKWOOD, No. 839 BROADWAY, NEW YORK.

Above: *The Class of 1863, shown here shortly before graduation, entered the Academy at the height of the Civil War. Of the fifty-nine original cadets, thirty-four failed to graduate. Half of those who dropped out joined the Confederate army.*

USMA Archives

Left: *During the difficult period of the Civil War, cadets could be seen wearing black bands of mourning.*

USMA Archives

battles, and a West Pointer commanded one side in the remaining five engagements. Academy-trained engineers, North and South, also handled the staggering logistical demands of the armies in the fields by surveying and building roads, railways, bridges, and telegraph lines.

Jefferson Davis, Class of 1828, who had narrowly escaped dismissal from the Academy for his clandestine visits to Benny Havens's tavern, became the first—and only—president of the Confederate States of America. Former superintendent and 1838 graduate P. G. T. Beauregard, now a general in the Confederate army, gave the order to open fire on Fort Sumter, and Wade Hampton Gibbes, who had fought with fellow cadet Emory Upton over a question of honor, manned one of the cannon. Commanding the fort's defenses was Major Robert Anderson, a graduate and former artillery instructor at the Academy.

Three months after Sumter, Beauregard soundly defeated his classmate Irvin McDowell in the war's first major land engagement along Bull Run near Manassas, Virginia. In that same battle Thomas Jackson, who had left his teaching position at VMI to lead a brigade of Virginia volunteer troops, demonstrated the same grim determination he had shown in his cadet days. Facing a strong attack by federal troops, he refused to retreat, earning the nickname he would carry for the rest of his life and long after his death—Stonewall Jackson.

George McClellan, the shining star of the Class of 1846, became the North's first war hero for his role in clearing western Virginia of

Jefferson Davis, president of the Confederate States of America, was an 1828 graduate of the U.S. Military Academy.

© Bettmann/CORBIS

This small flag fragment from Fort Sumter was given by Major Robert Anderson, Class of 1825, to the Women's Volunteer Relief Association of Livingston City to help raise money for wounded soldiers.

West Point Museum Collections, USMA

This saddle with pistols, valise, and saddlecloth belonged to Major General John Sedgwick, Class of 1837, a veteran of many battles in the Mexican and Civil Wars. He was killed in the battle of Spotsylvania in 1864.

its meager Confederate garrison. In the wake of the Bull Run disaster, Lincoln appointed him commanding general of the Union's largest fighting force, the Army of the Potomac. McClellan proved to be an able organizer, instilling discipline and pride in the raw amateur soldiers who made up his ranks. On the battlefield, however, he exhibited a timorous nature coupled with a tendency to grossly overestimate the enemy's strength. His lack of drive eventually forced Lincoln to remove him from command. Running as the Democratic Party's candidate for president against Lincoln in 1864, McClellan was soundly defeated.

Emory Upton, still bearing the scar on his face acquired during the barracks brawl with Gibbes, rose through the ranks on the basis of his laudable wartime service to become a brevet major general. At various times he commanded an artillery battery, an infantry division, and a cavalry division. After the war he would be appointed to the post of commandant of cadets at his alma mater.

Robert E. Lee's role as the Confederacy's foremost commander and one of the ablest generals America has ever produced is the stuff of legends. Even though he fought on the losing side, Lee has been enshrined in the pantheon of the country's greatest military heroes. He inspired unwavering, even reverential devotion among his officers and men—and dread in those northern generals who opposed him. Only one Union commander seemed uncowed by the prospect of facing Robert E. Lee, an old comrade in arms from the Mexican War days.

Ulysses S. Grant had compiled an impressive record in the western theater during the first three years of the war. In February 1862 at Fort Donelson in Tennessee, he besieged a Confederate force commanded by Simon Bolivar Buckner, West Point Class of 1844 and one of Grant's closest friends before the war. When Buckner sent him a dispatch asking for the terms of capitulation, Grant wrote back, "No terms except an unconditional and immediate surrender can be accepted. I propose to move immediately upon your works."

Grant had gone on to engineer the capture of Vicksburg and the stunning Union victory at Chattanooga before Lincoln called him east in the spring of 1864 to lead the Army of the Potomac in a decisive campaign against the Confederate capital of Richmond. Lee's army blocked Grant's path in a densely wooded corner of Virginia known as the Wilderness. As he had done against all previous adversaries, Lee appeared to be gaining the upper hand. A frightened officer rushed up to Grant crying that Lee was about to cut the army off

Although Robert E. Lee was offered command of the Union's field forces, he declined the command. After his home state of Virginia seceded, he resigned his commission in the U.S. Army and joined Virginia's fledging military force.

Office of Notary Public

Rockbridge County, Va., *October 2nd* 1865.

AMNESTY OATH.

I *Robert E. Lee* of *Lexington Virginia* do solemnly swear, in the presence of Almighty God, that I will henceforth faithfully support, protect and defend the Constitution of the *United States*, and the *Union* of the States thereunder, and that I will, in like manner, abide by and faithfully support all laws and proclamations which have been made during the existing rebellion with reference to the emancipation of slaves, so help me God.

R E Lee

Sworn to and subscribed before me, this *2nd* day of *October* 1865.

Chas. A. Davidson NOTARY PUBLIC.

from its lines of communications. "Oh, I am heartily tired of hearing what Lee is going to do," Grant snapped. "Some of you always seem to think he is suddenly going to turn a double somersault and land in our rear and on both of our flanks at the same time. Go back to your command, and try to think what we are going to do ourselves, instead of what Lee is going to do."

Grant eventually extricated his army from the Wilderness and relentlessly pushed on toward Richmond. Lee was forced to dig miles of trench lines to defend the besieged capital. It was a contest in which he could not hope to prevail against the North's superior manpower and matériel. Finally, in April 1865, he abandoned Richmond and moved his tattered, shrinking army west, hoping to escape. But Grant pressed his troops forward night and day, and they finally cornered Lee at the peaceful country village of Appomattox Court House.

The proud, stoic Virginian at long last faced the inevitable and sent Grant a note asking for surrender terms—perhaps remembering with apprehension the Union commander's reply at Fort Donelson. But this time Grant responded that his only

After the end of the Civil War, Lee signed this statement reaffirming his loyalty to the U.S. Constitution. He devoted the rest of his life to setting an example of conduct for other ex-Confederates.

condition was that Confederate soldiers lay down their arms and promise not to take them up again. A meeting was arranged at a nearby farmhouse, and Lee rode forward at the appointed hour. A Union officer later recalled, "I turned about, and there behind me, riding between my two lines, appeared a commanding form, superbly mounted, richly accoutered, of imposing bearing, noble countenance, with expression of deep sadness overmastered by deeper strength. It is no other than Robert E. Lee! And seen by me for the first time within my own lines. I sat immovable, with a certain awe and admiration."

Grant had ridden hard for hours over muddy roads to reach the farmhouse. He carried no sword and was wearing a private's tunic with lieutenant general's stars sewn on the shoulders. As he

Lieutenant General Ulysses S. Grant relaxes at camp in Cold Harbor, Virginia, 1864.

" OH, I AM HEARTILY TIRED OF HEARING WHAT LEE IS GOING TO DO, GO BACK TO YOUR COMMAND, AND TRY TO THINK WHAT WE ARE GOING TO DO OURSELVES, INSTEAD OF WHAT LEE IS GOING TO DO."

— U L Y S S E S   S .   G R A N T

dismounted and started up the steps, Grant recalled the episode at Scott's headquarters in Mexico so long ago. To break the ice after formal introductions were concluded, he mentioned the incident to Lee. "Yes, I know I met you on that occasion," Lee replied politely, "and I have often thought of it, and tried to recollect how you looked, but I have never been able to recall a single feature."

After a few minutes of small talk, the two generals turned to the business at hand. Grant reiterated his conditions and promised that Confederate soldiers returning to their homes would not be disturbed by federal authorities. A relieved Lee observed, "This will have a very happy effect on my army." After the surrender documents had been signed, Lee and Grant shook hands and parted company. Within a few days Lee returned to war-torn Richmond, where his ailing wife, Mary, awaited him. Grant hurried off to Washington to a hero's welcome.

Thus did these two products of the U. S. Military Academy conclude the nation's

most costly and divisive conflict. Lieutenant Morris Schaff, Class of 1862, who had experienced the horrors of war with Grant in the Wilderness, wrote, "Those two West Point men knew the ideals of their old Alma Mater, they knew each other as only graduates of that institution know each other, and they met on the plane of that common knowledge." Seldom if ever in human history has a civil war ended on such a conciliatory note. There would be no reprisals, no hangings; the country could move ahead with the long, slow process of healing its deep wounds.

At West Point Cadet Charles King described the victory celebration following Appomattox as a "thunderous uproar that bellowed along the Hudson the soft April day that brought us tidings of the close of the war." He added, "All the batteries turned loose at once, and presently the gray battlements of the beautiful old Point were wreathed in sulfur smoke."

In Richmond, meanwhile, the reconciliation had already begun. A few days after the surrender, Union Major General Godfrey Weitzel, commanding the federal forces that occupied the city, handed a purse full of money to an aide. He then ordered the man to "go to General Lee's house, find Fitzhugh Lee, and say that his old West Point chum Godfrey Weitzel wishes to know if he needs anything, and urge him to take what he may need from that pocketbook."

Above: *Richard Norris Brooke's painting depicts Confederate soldiers at Appomattox furling their flag for a final time.*

CHAPTER FIVE

1865—1902

A TIME
of TROUBLES

Near the end of 1865, some seven months

after the end of the Civil War, a small group of Second Classmen decided to form their

own billiard club. Their endeavor violated regulations and thus had to proceed in the

utmost secrecy. They had a new billiard table shipped up to Garrison from

New York City. Then, under cover of night, the conspirators carted their

prize across the frozen river using a team and sled temporarily appropriated

from the mess steward. They installed the table in a cellar room hidden by

the coal bunkers under C Company barracks. They boarded up the

windows and insulated them with tanbark to deaden the sound of clicking

billiard balls. A number of accoutrements, including a heat stove, kerosene

lamps, a keg of cider, a barrel of crackers, and a whole cheese, completed

their subterranean clubhouse.

 A chance event a few weeks later threatened to close down the

clandestine club. The voucher from the manufacturer acknowledging

payment for the billiard table somehow found its way into the office of the

Academy treasurer. He alerted tactical officers, who undertook a full-scale search for this

contraband. They looked in the barracks attic, basement washrooms, and nearby houses,

but without success. The club thrived and grew to some thirty members.

 Officers remained on the alert, however, and their vigilance paid off nearly a year

later. One night a pair of them spotted two suspicious-looking cadets clad in bathrobes

and slippers and followed them down the barracks stairs and through the coal bins.

Nearby they heard the click of billiard balls. The officers decided to wait and summon

reinforcements for a raid the following night. A cadet happened to overhear their plans,

and he alerted other club members.

West Point Museum Collections, USMA

Old carbide-style brass lamps like these two were used in the Mess Hall from 1850 to 1929. The lamps are missing their glass globes.

At the end of the Civil War, the Academy's rigid atmosphere and limitations on social activities were eased.

The club assembled the following morning and decided to go out in style. Members would "make a virtue out of necessity," wrote one of them, Cadet Oliver E. Wood, "and yield in a handsome manner." They cleaned up the room, polished the lamps, lit a fire in the stove, and left a note on the table next to the carefully racked balls. That night, shortly after Taps, nearly all the officers on duty assembled in the guardroom and marched to the club. They forced open the door and found the note bequeathing them the table "as a slight token of our gratitude . . . in allowing us for so long a time to enjoy the privilege of the Club." The officers, to their embarrassment, never did learn the names of the conspirators. They were "for a long time," Oliver Wood noted, "twitted by the ladies at their grand failure in 'hiving' the cadets."

The great billiard escapade reflected the Academy's loosened atmosphere following the taut years of the Civil War. In subsequent decades the cadets undertook new entertainments, both authorized and illicit. In 1881, on the one hundredth night before graduation, First Classmen staged an entertainment with songs, skits, and readings mocking themselves, officers, and even the superintendent. At this Hundredth Night show, the special guest was Samuel Clemens, who wrote under the name Mark Twain. A resident of Hartford, Connecticut, Twain became a frequent visitor who could be seen sauntering around the post, chewing on a cigar, and swapping stories with cadets.

The influence of the Civil War and its aftermath was felt in other ways. The Battle Monument finally erected there in 1897, forty-two years after the war, would honor the Union dead—2,230 soldiers and officers of the regular army. But surprisingly, reconciliation among the living proceeded more rapidly at West Point than in the nation at large. Young men from the Confederate states were admitted to the plebe class as early as 1868. The following year, graduates met to form an alumni association—the Association of Graduates—that would soon embrace northern and southern veterans alike, gathering annually to remember their cadet days and relish old war stories.

A less surprising legacy of the war at West Point was a kind of self-satisfaction. The Academy could take

Above: *Battle Monument, located at scenic Trophy Point, has long been one of the most visited spots on the West Point campus. The monument lists the names of 2,230 soldiers and officers of the regular army killed in action in the Civil War.*
© Ted Spiegel

Left: *Cadets entertain a guest at the monument circa 1902.*
Library of Congress

GRADUATES UNITE TO FOSTER HEALING

*D*uring the summer of 1864, Confederate General George Pickett's wife gave birth to a baby boy. When news of this event reached the Union army, General Grant and other West Pointers commemorated the birth by purchasing a children's silver tea set and sending it through the lines. "Who can conceive of something like that happening in the middle of a war," says Professor Carol Reardon, military historian at the Pennsylvania State University, "if it weren't for the ties that were forged at West Point?"

Unfortunately, however, the Academy was not spared the divisions that plagued the country during the Civil War. During the prewar years, cadets from the North and South had bonded as classmates, but by 1865 several classes had graduated with no southern cadets at all. Even when young men from the former Confederate states began returning to the Academy in 1868, obstacles of sectional prejudice and suspicion had to be overcome. "That was a difficult period for the Academy," says Lieutenant General Daniel W. Christman, former superintendent of West Point. "It took about two decades before the rupture that the war represented to our nation was healed here at the Academy."

Lieutenant General Daniel W. Christman

One of the ways that the healing started to take place was through the formation of the Association of Graduates (AOG). Founded in 1869, it began as a small fraternal organization for all living USMA graduates. Initially, its purpose was to reunite Academy graduates after the Civil War. During the 1870s, as an annual ceremony, "cadets of both Union armies and the Confederacy gathered on the Plain," says Christman, "and in a spirit of reconciliation brought the alumni back together again, symbolizing the unity of this school after the country had reunified."

Until the end of World War II, the AOG remained a fraternal and social organization. As the USMA moved into the post–Vietnam War period, with the increase in the size of the Corps of Cadets and with burgeoning financial needs, the AOG transformed from a social fellowship into a viable independent nonprofit organization. Its fund-raising program sought private solicitations to help defray the cost of projects for which appropriated funds were not available.

Today the Association of Graduates serves as the alumni association of the U.S. Military Academy. Its mission is to further the ideals and promote the welfare of West Point.

Alumni Review on the Plain.

© Bob Krist

pride in having produced the great generals on both sides—Lee and Jackson as well as Grant and Sherman. Basking in their glory, Academy faculty and officials concluded that they must indeed be doing something right. They became so reluctant to revise the curriculum that some later historians would label the period as one of stagnation. The reluctance to alter course was expressed soon after the war by Superintendent George W. Cullum. In 1866, upon hearing vague rumors that Congress might propose some changes at the Academy, Cullum wrote a U.S. senator that a system "which for half a century has borne such prolific fruits of excellence, should not be lightly changed for any new patent nostrums. Leave well enough alone is a wise saying."

The Academy's adherence to the status quo contrasted sharply with the ferment bubbling up in most American colleges during the latter half of the nineteenth century. They abandoned the rigid classical approach to instruction and introduced radically new ideas. These included a preference for specialized education, with programs of graduate study and electives to be chosen by the student. The motive was to keep pace with the accelerating intellectual and technological developments of the time. Defenders of West Point pointed out that the Academy had jettisoned the classical approach from its beginning. Content with the existing curriculum, they echoed the conservatism of Superintendent Thomas Ruger, who reported in

" THE SUBJECTS OF STUDY AT THE MILITARY ACADEMY EMBRACE ALL THAT IS ESSENTIAL AND NEARLY ALL THAT IS NECESSARY TO THE EDUCATION OF AN OFFICER OF THE ARMY."

— SUPERINTENDENT THOMAS RUGER

1872: "The subjects of study at the Military Academy embrace all that is essential and nearly all that is necessary to the education of an officer of the Army."

In comparative terms, the Academy seemed to lag most noticeably in the course of study that traditionally had been its strongest—engineering. For decades West Point had turned out the nation's leading engineers. Working as architects, surveyors, and engineers in the service of the army and civilian enterprises, its graduates had built much of the nation's infrastructure, from the harbors and canals of the Northeast to the railroads that were spanning the West. After the Civil War, however, other specialized institutions gradually overtook West Point in engineering eminence—albeit with a strong leg up from the Academy. Of the nineteen U.S. technical colleges operating in 1870, ten could trace their ancestry to West Point graduates.

Other factors besides the rise of specialized civilian institutions accounted for the relative decline of West Point engineering. An 1866 congressional measure removed control of the Academy from the Army Corps of Engineers and, for the first time, enabled the superintendent to be a member of any branch, not just the Corps. The engineering department itself resisted change. The department head, Dennis Hart Mahan, began as an instructor in 1830 and served for forty-one years under eleven different superintendents until his death in 1871, when—distraught over impending retirement—he either jumped or accidentally fell overboard from a Hudson paddle steamer.

USMA Archives

Dennis Hart Mahan taught engineering at the Academy for more than four decades.

Longtime professors like Mahan and his colleague Albert Church, who taught math for half a century, wielded enormous power. They remained members of the academic board, which controlled curriculum, while superintendents came and went. Superintendents usually served tours of less than five years after the position was changed in 1839 from permanent, as it had been under Sylvanus Thayer, to temporary. The superintendent possessed just one of the votes on the academic board, even when he brought high rank to the job. Major General John M. Schofield, the former secretary of war who was no less than the third ranking officer in the army when he was appointed superintendent in 1876, still had to battle within the board for influence over curriculum. The professors were civilians, not officers, and he could not simply give them orders. Even the acknowledged father of the Academy, Thayer himself, was rebuffed when he recommended from retirement a thorough overhaul of the curriculum he had helped create. Only at West Point, it was later observed, could professors "boast that there [had] been no substantial change in the curriculum since 1840."

> " LIKE THE HOUSE THAT DEFIED THE STORM, WEST POINT IS BUILT ON A ROCK AND THAT ROCK IS MATHEMATICS."
>
> — A WEST POINT PROFESSOR

Though instruction in the humanities gradually increased, mathematics remained the bedrock of the curriculum. "Like the house that defied the storm, West Point is built on a rock," averred one professor, "and that rock is mathematics." Late in the century, someone calculated, cadets spent on mathematics no fewer than 213,495 minutes of classroom time and preparation against 239,720 minutes for all other subjects. This was nearly twice the time expended on math as at Yale, Harvard, and Massachusetts Institute of Technology. Thayer in his day had justified the massive doses of math as essential for officers in engineering and artillery. Increasingly, as

the historians Joseph Ellis and Robert Moore noted, they were rationalized as "a form of intellectual exercise that improved the strength and tone of one's mental muscles."

The most direct consequence of the Civil War was the tumultuous attempt to racially integrate West Point. Under Reconstruction, the states of the former Confederacy were controlled by the federal government, and Radical Republicans in particular pressed for the rights of newly liberated blacks. In 1867 Congressman Benjamin F. Butler of Massachusetts began seeking African American candidates for West Point. He sought help from James Fairchild, the president of Ohio's Oberlin College, a pioneer in integration of both blacks and women. Neither man could come up with a candidate he felt combined physical and academic qualifications together with the kind of rugged constitution that would be required by a trailblazer breaking tradition at the military bastion on the Hudson.

Three years later, in 1870, the first black deemed to possess these qualifications was admitted to the Academy. James Webster Smith, the son of a free-born mother and a former

Members of the staff and faculty of the U.S. Military Academy in 1870. Civilian professors during this period had significant influence and power and often did battle with the superintendent over the curriculum.

slave who became a prosperous carpenter, was appointed by a South Carolina congressman, Solomon I. Hoge, one of the so-called carpetbaggers—northerners who had gone South to take advantage of Reconstruction. Smith, a tall, slim youth, was well prepared academically. He had been befriended by a Connecticut philanthropist who brought him to Hartford to finish high school and sent him to Howard University. "The sudden intrusion of this negro into the West Point system may work a great deal that is bad," observed a correspondent of the *Boston Globe*, "but I believe, from what I have seen and heard, that if people who are not prejudiced look at the thing in its proper light there need be no fear of A NATIONAL CATASTROPHE from the innovation."

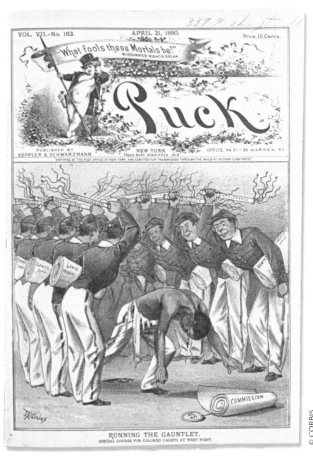

"Running the Gauntlet. Special Course for Colored Cadets at West Point" by J. A. Wales, 1880.

Smith was immediately ostracized by the white cadets. He was given a room alone; the father of a fellow plebe had expressed great enthusiasm for racial integration until an officer suggested his son might want to room with Smith. Cadets assigned to Smith's mess table applied for transfer to another table. Superintendent Thomas Pitcher refused the requests and had two of the cadets arrested for refusing to sit with Smith. In an account published later, Smith noted that within an hour after reporting to the Academy he was reminded by several cadets that he was not welcome. While he slept, a cadet threw the contents of a slop pail on his bed. Though Academy authorities treated him correctly for the most part, some officers were at pains to conceal their dislike. Some considered him part of a conspiracy by the abolitionists to destroy the institution. Tactical officer Rufus King later wrote of his "little beady, snake-like eyes" and characterized him as "the personification of repulsive gloom."

In the face of social banishment, taunts, and outright contempt, Smith showed open defiance. He refused to back down in encounters with whites and got into brawls. After ranking tenth in his plebe class, he plunged into academic decline. A letter to his benefactor complaining about treatment from other cadets and accusing the academic board of rigging entrance examinations against black candidates appeared in the *Hartford Courant* and other newspapers. A court of inquiry, including two general officers, began an investigation. Congressmen, reporters, and churchwomen descended upon the post. President Ulysses S. Grant—the first Academy graduate to serve as chief executive—even intervened on his behalf. Twice Smith underwent a court-martial; he was forced to repeat his plebe year. His struggle finally ended after four years when he was dismissed for failing to pass an examination in natural and experimental philosophy, as physics was then called.

The attitudes and behavior of Smith's roommate during his last year presented a sharp contrast. Like Smith, Henry Ossian Flipper was a former southern slave with a solid academic background. He came from a strong family and was the appointee of a Georgia Republican congressman. But unlike Smith, Flipper entered West Point determined at all costs to keep a low profile and avoid antagonizing white cadets. Even before traveling to the post, he refused to cooperate with a Georgia newspaper that wanted to publicize his appointment; he feared "too great a knowledge of me should precede me." He wrote later in his autobiography: "From the day I entered till the day I graduated I had not cause to utter so much as an angry word. I refused to obtrude myself upon the white cadets, and treated them all with uniform courtesy. I have been treated likewise." In fact, the "uniform courtesy" with which he was treated consisted of silence and contempt. "We don't have anything to do with him off duty," a cadet told a Philadelphia reporter. "We don't even speak to him."

Flipper's own personal philosophy of gradualism in race relations helped him endure indignities and insults with a steely resolve. He refused to report them to the authorities. He criticized those on the outside who were calling on Congress to protect black cadets. "If my

USMA Archives

In 1877 Henry Ossian Flipper became the first African American to graduate from the U.S. Military Academy.

" IF MY MANHOOD CANNOT STAND WITHOUT A GOVERNMENTAL PROP, THEN LET IT FALL. IF I AM TO STAND ON ANY OTHER GROUND THAN THE ONE WHITE CADETS STAND UPON, THEN I DON'T WANT THE CADETSHIP."

— HENRY OSSIAN FLIPPER

manhood cannot stand without a governmental prop, then let it fall. If I am to stand on any other ground than the one white cadets stand upon, then I don't want the cadetship. If I cannot endure prejudice and persecutions, even if they are offered, then I don't deserve the cadetship, and much less the commission of an army officer."

Mistreatment of blacks, he believed, originated with that minority of cadets who come "from the very lowest classes of our population." In his view these cadets, "uncouth and rough in appearance," ruled the Corps by fear. "Indeed I know there are many who would associate, who would treat me as a brother cadet, were they not held in constant dread of this class." He cited examples of classmates who, when no one else was present, would express regret at his treatment.

The "Buffalo Soldiers" were first assigned to West Point in 1907 to support cadet riding instruction and mounted drill. They remained at the Academy until they were deactivated in 1946.

© Underwood & Underwood/CORBIS

By his final year Flipper proudly noted that he regularly heard himself called "Mr. Flipper." Though some cadets were shocked when they saw him serving as officer of the guard, they nonetheless recognized his authority. In 1877 Flipper became the first African American to graduate from the Military Academy. He was fiftieth in a class of seventy-six, and the only graduate to be greeted with cheers. Cadets went to the room where he had lived alone and in silence like a monk to shake his hand. "All signs of ostracism were gone," he wrote. "All felt I was worthy of some regard, and did not fail to extend it to me."

Now the U.S. Army's first and only black commissioned officer, Second Lieutenant Flipper was assigned to the Tenth Cavalry Regiment on the Southwest frontier. This outfit— composed of black enlisted men and, until Flipper, only white officers—had compiled such a

After graduation Flipper was convicted of conduct unbecoming an officer and dishonorably discharged from the military. It was a racially motivated case, and more than a century later, President Bill Clinton, pictured here with Flipper's great-grandnephew, pardoned Flipper.

first-rate combat record against the Plains Indians that they respectfully referred to members as Buffalo Soldiers. Flipper's duties included supervising the construction of a telegraph line and a drainage system at Fort Sill known as Flipper's Ditch, which eliminated the problem of stagnant water and the threat of malaria. At Fort Davis, Texas, however, he ran into problems. He was accused of mishandling commissary

© AFP/CORBIS

funds. Some evidence, including his open friendship with the sister-in-law of his troop commander, suggested he may have been singled out because of race. A court-martial acquitted him of embezzlement but convicted him of conduct unbecoming an officer. He was dishonorably discharged from the army in 1882.

Undeterred, Flipper went on to become an expert surveyor, mapmaker, and civil and mining engineer; he recorded his adventures in a memoir, *Black Frontiersman.* He served as a special agent for the Justice Department, an expert on Mexico for the Senate Foreign Relations Committee, and an assistant to the secretary of the interior. But the court-martial, carried out under such questionable circumstances, haunted him and his supporters. In 1976, thirty-six years after his death, the army reversed his dishonorable discharge; in 1999 President Bill Clinton pardoned Henry Ossian Flipper, whose memory West Point honors with an award given annually to the cadet who demonstrates leadership, self-discipline, and perseverance in light of unusual difficulties.

Soon after Flipper's graduation from West Point, the trail he had blazed there with such iron restraint had turned bleak. Another black cadet, Johnson C. Whittaker, the South Carolina successor to the ousted Smith, encountered problems almost immediately. He won opprobrium by reporting—instead of turning the other cheek as the unwritten rule would dictate—a white cadet who had struck him in the face during an altercation. Then, in 1879, he barely escaped dismissal for academic deficiency. Superintendent John Schofield instead turned him back a year, saying Whittaker had "won the sympathy of all by his manly deportment and earnest efforts to succeed."

Following the graduation of a few African American cadets in the years after the Civil War, it would be forty years before the Military Academy would see another. Today racial and ethnic minorities represent 15 to 20 percent of the Corps of Cadets.

© Ted Spiegel

Schofield was hoping to avoid the public turmoil that had attended the Smith case, but an even larger cause célèbre erupted the following year. One morning an officer found Whittaker lying on the floor of his room with hands and feet bound, his head bloodied, and an Indian club nearby. Whittaker said he had been attacked by three masked men during the previous night. His wounds proved to be superficial, and investigators soon concluded they were self-inflicted. Handwriting experts concluded that a note of warning

" I DO NOT BELIEVE WEST POINT IS THE PLACE TO TRY THE EXPERIMENT OF SOCIAL EQUALITY."

—ARMY COMMANDER IN CHIEF WILLIAM T. SHERMAN

Whittaker said he had received before the incident actually had been written by Whittaker himself. Amid a storm of national publicity, a court of inquiry and then a court-martial determined that Whittaker had staged the incident, allegedly to divert attention from his academic difficulties.

President Chester A. Arthur overturned the decision. This provoked outrage from the army commander in chief, William T. Sherman, who denounced the president and the press for acting "like a pack of hounds barking at they knew not what." Schofield, writing to his old friend Sherman, described the president's intervention as political—"for the purpose, hardly attempted to be disguised, of alluring the colored vote." In the end Whittaker was dismissed for academic deficiency.

The Whittaker case stirred a strong popular clamor for the removal of Schofield. The superintendent was bitter. He felt he had demonstrated "undue kindness toward an unworthy cadet for no better reason than that he is colored." So soon after their emergence from slavery, he said, it was unreasonable to expect "Negroes to compete with whites, and a mistake to make them try." The secretary of war, without consulting Sherman, relieved Schofield as superintendent and replaced him with General Oliver O. Howard. As head of the Freedmen's Bureau and founder of Howard University, Howard enjoyed an irreproachable reputation among blacks and was selected primarily for that reason. Sherman, however, considered Howard "extreme on this question." He wrote Howard, "I do not believe West Point is the place to try the experiment of social equality."

Howard served less than two years and was not around when two black cadets successfully followed the path of Henry Flipper. In the Class of 1887, John H. Alexander quietly placed in the middle—thirty-second out of sixty-four graduates—without

Oliver O. Howard, known for his work with freed slaves, was named superintendent of the Military Academy in 1881.

RETURN OF THE PRODIGAL SON

George Armstrong Custer was disarmingly candid about his days at West Point. "My career as a cadet had but little to recommend it to the study of those who came after," he wrote later, "unless as an example to be carefully avoided." The fun-loving Custer seemed never to be able to pass up the temptation to talk in the ranks, throw snowballs at a passing column, play forbidden games of cards, or lead a late-night foray to Benny Havens. Once he stole a tactical officer's rooster, cooked the bird, and served it to his classmates.

He was usually in academic trouble as well. Facing failure in one course, he broke into the instructor's quarters to copy exam questions from a book. When he heard someone coming, he ripped out the page and fled. The instructor, seeing a page missing, changed the exam. Custer squeaked by anyway. He graduated in 1861 last in his class academically and tops in demerits; he had amassed a four-year total of no fewer than 726. "He is one of the best-hearted and cleverest men that I ever knew," wrote a roommate, Tully McCrea. "The great difficulty is that he is too clever for his own good."

During the Civil War, Custer's gallantry in the Union cavalry won him promotion to brevet brigadier general at age twenty-five. Later the flamboyant "boy general" was assigned to the Indian wars on the Western frontier, where his dashing career ended at the Battle of Little Bighorn. In 1877 the remains of this prodigal son were returned to West Point and buried with full honors from the Corps of Cadets. A bronze statue of Custer was dedicated two years later on a knoll across from the mess hall. Congress had authorized the melting down of twenty bronze cannon for casting the statue, and Custer stood larger than life—his long hair flowing, a saber in one hand and a pistol in the other. Custer's widow, Libby, did not attend the dedication. She had not been consulted about the sculpture and objected to the full-dress uniform as improper, the face as too old, and the weaponry as excessive—he "is armed like a desperado in both hands."

For years Libby Custer tried unsuccessfully to get West Point to remove the statue. Finally, in 1884, Secretary of War Robert Lincoln agreed. The base was removed and placed on Custer's grave. The statue itself was stored in a supply shed, from which it eventually disappeared without a trace. Later speculation suggested that it may have found its way, along with other West Point relics, into a scrap-metal drive during World War II.

Left: *The base of Custer's missing statue now crowns the top of his grave at West Point.*
Library of Congress

Right: *Just before riding into the valley of Little Bighorn on June 25, 1876, Custer sent this message to his subordinate, Captain Frederick Benteen. The dispatch, written by Custer's adjutant, William W. Cooke, reads: "Benteen. Come on. Big village. Be quick. Bring packs. W. W. Cooke. P.S. Bring pacs."*
West Point Museum Collections, USMA

generating undue national attention. Another black, Charles D. Young, failed the engineering exam in 1889, but his instructor made a special plea to tutor him for reexamination. It turned out to be one of several successes for the instructor, Lieutenant George Goethals, who later served as the hard-driving chief engineer for construction of the Panama Canal. Young passed the retest, graduated that summer to the delight of classmates who praised "his patient perseverance in the face of discouraging conditions," and rose to the rank of colonel before his retirement.

Young would be the last African American to graduate for nearly five decades. In those years before the end of the nineteenth century, the nation lost its passion for racial integration. In the South, Reconstruction was dead and, with the acquiescence of the North, new state measures known as Jim Crow laws were lending legitimacy to rigid segregation of the races. West Point had admitted a dozen African Americans and graduated three. To some historians looking back a century later, it was insufficient. "Preservation of the legal rights of these first black cadets was not enough; strict guardianship of their human rights was the only proper course," wrote Scott Dillard during the 1970s. "West Point had the opportunity to stand as a bulwark and had abdicated the responsibility." Others noted that during the period in question the Naval Academy did not admit, let alone graduate, a single black midshipman.

No single problem, not even racial integration, troubled West Point more in the decades after the Civil War than the practice of hazing. Upperclassmen had always been prone to playing pranks on new cadets, especially at summer camp. Known in the early days as deviling, this for the most part consisted of harmless mischief of the kind inflicted on neophytes by experienced campers. After the war, however, hazing took on new and sinister forms of physical and psychological harassment that sometimes resulted in pain and suffering. (Blacks were almost never actually hazed, but left strictly

USMA Archives

alone.) By the end of the nineteenth century, hazing had become so embedded in West Point culture—and so notorious in the nation's press—that it threatened the very existence of the Academy.

Precisely why the practice burgeoned and built to a crisis during this period is not clear. Some historians traced it to the war itself. During the fighting, many soldiers from the ranks were admitted to the Academy; they were rough hewn, experienced in the sometimes abusive give-and-take of ordinary army life. Then, too, veteran officers returning to West Point after the war tended to be less inclined to enforce regulations they considered petty compared to their wartime experiences, contributing to an atmosphere of lax discipline. Historian James Blackwell blamed the lack of other entertainments. "The only diversions cadets had were those they invented themselves," he wrote. "In this environment hazing became a high art form."

The upsurge in harassment coincided with a new form of orientation for plebes introduced after the war and soon known as the Beast Barracks. Formerly, new cadets went directly into summer camp; now introduction to West Point life began during three or more weeks of segregation in the barracks. They were attended there by a few upperclassmen assigned to teach them saluting, marching, and other military basics. The older cadets typically seized the opportunity to deflate the newcomers of any sense of self-importance, since plebes often were the best athletes and smartest students in their hometowns. They subjected them to the exaggerated, shoulders-back, chin-in posture

known as the brace, berated them with names like Thing, Animal, or Mr. Dumbjohn and screamed at them day and night. Plebes were forced to perform strenuous physical exercises such as the repeated deep knee bends known as eagling (because the arms flapped like a bird attempting to take flight) or swimming to Newburgh—lying facedown on dry ground and thrashing about with arms and legs. One particularly humiliating exercise required the plebe to stand on his head naked in a bathtub filled with water.

One of America's most famous army officers, John J. Pershing, graduated from West Point in 1886. As an upperclassman he was known for his hazing of younger cadets.

After Beast Barracks, harassment continued and sometimes intensified at summer camp. Upperclassmen seldom allowed the exhausted plebes to rest. At night they would perform "foot inspection"—dripping hot candle wax onto the blistered feet of the sleeping plebes. Or they would yank them out of their blankets and throw them into the drainage ditch alongside the camp. Even on guard duty plebes were not immune to hazing. Older cadets wearing sheets to appear ghostly—and not incidentally to shield their identity—pounced on them and roughed them up.

Summer camp was also typically the occasion for beginning the year-round practice of making virtual servants out of plebes. Upperclassmen ordered them to make their beds, polish their swords, or clean their living areas. A tall, rangy upperclassman from Missouri named John J. Pershing was notorious for ordering plebes to police the area in front of his tent. This future commander in chief of the Allied Expeditionary Force during World War I was cadet captain in 1886, his final year. According to another cadet, Robert Lee Bullard, Pershing exercised authority with "a nature peculiarly impersonal, dispassionate, hard and firm." Pershing invented the so-called string trick, which he orchestrated to the amusement of upperclassmen. He would gather a score or more of plebes in the company street and order them to count off. When he moved his arm to pull an imaginary string in one direction, the odd-numbered cadets thrust an arm out at a stiff right angle. When he pulled the string in the opposite direction, they dropped their arms and the even-numbered cadets thrust a leg out. If a tactical officer happened by, Pershing simply dropped his pretend string, ending this live marionette show, and then began drilling the plebes.

Harassment of first-year men came to be considered the prerogative of upper-class cadets for their own amusement and for the purported benefits it bestowed upon the plebes. Exposing these young officers-to-be to extreme stress, it was reasoned, toughened them up and weeded out those who were unfit to serve. Alumni largely supported hazing; after all, they had endured it without apparent injury and supposedly to their benefit. Many likened it to a primitive rite of passage —a coming-of-age ritual—that prepared the tribe's warriors. In his study of hazing at West Point, *Bullies and Cowards*, historian Philip W. Leon pointed out that, in contrast with the yearlong harassment of first-year cadets, "archetypal initiation rituals usually lasted only a few days." Ancient rituals, moreover, were regulated and codified by "the collective wisdom and experience of the larger organization." At West Point, Leon added, "random hazers in the corps of cadets created their own authority for their individual acts of cruelty."

Practically all plebes submitted to hazing without formal complaint. Some welcomed the attention as a break from the isolation imposed during the first years. Others saw it as an opportunity to win the approval and acceptance of their peers as well as their betters. Most refused to report incidents because they feared speaking up would simply bring even more misery down upon them. Occasionally plebes would retaliate in some small way.

© Robert Stewart

A strict set of rules governs cadet life during Cadet Basic Training and throughout the first academic year. Here, a plebe receives instruction from an older cadet.

Members of the Class of 1879, forced to polish the swords of upperclassmen, later told of pouring water into the scabbards so the weapons would rust.

The same risk of intimidation that threatened plebes also affected upperclassmen who openly opposed harassment. In 1875 Charles Robinson, a Third Classman, reported an instance of a plebe performing menial service for a member of the First Class. Robinson was "cut"—left in silence—by both the First Class and his own Third Class. The ordeal took its toll; at the end of his final year, he was found deficient in academics and dismissed.

Academy officials rarely could prevail upon plebes to identify the upperclassmen tormenting them. This difficulty was illustrated during a congressional hearing into hazing in 1901 in the following exchange with Cadet Douglas MacArthur.

Congressman: Was it too dark for you to recognize the faces of your hazers?
MacArthur: I do not think it would have been if I had looked at them, but it is generally customary for Fourth Class men not to look at those people who are hazing them.

As plebes, MacArthur and other sons of prominent men, especially generals, were favorite targets of upperclassmen. Philip H. Sheridan Jr. was forced to ride a broomstick horse from one end of the street to the other in parody of his father, the illustrious cavalryman. MacArthur had to recite over and over again the Civil War exploits of his father, Arthur, a ranking army general. One night at summer camp, he was subjected to what cadets called a soiree—an exhausting medley of various hazing practices in one session. The session culminated in an exhausting full hour of eagling that led MacArthur to collapse and lie temporarily unable to move. In the congressional hearing he reluctantly conceded after much prompting that such treatment was cruel. "Hazing was practiced with a worthy goal," he wrote in his memoirs, "but with methods that were violent and uncontrolled."

The Sisyphean task of stamping out the practice generally fell to the superintendent, who looked in vain for help. Faculty often lent surreptitious support to hazing. Most alumni supported it openly. Though cadets found guilty of hazing were subject to mandatory dismissal, influential graduates in Congress or the War Department often succeeded in winning their reinstatement. Superintendents tried a variety of stratagems to stop hazing. They extracted oaths of obedience from upperclassmen who had to swear they would not harass entering cadets. Sometimes cadets going on furlough first had to sign a pledge that they had not "improperly interfered with, or molested, harassed, or injured new Cadets."

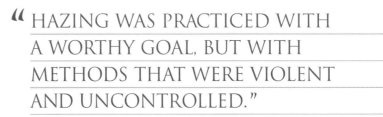

" HAZING WAS PRACTICED WITH A WORTHY GOAL, BUT WITH METHODS THAT WERE VIOLENT AND UNCONTROLLED."

— D O U G L A S   M A C A R T H U R

As a cadet,
Douglas MacArthur,
Class of 1903, was
the target of hazing
by upperclassmen.

In 1871, attempting to stem the postwar outbreak of hazing, President Grant personally selected as superintendent Colonel Thomas Howard Ruger, who was known as a strict disciplinarian. Ruger "tightened all the loose 'screws,'" wrote Cadet Tasker Bliss. When Cadet Hugh Scott was caught hazing a plebe, he was turned back a year. Not even when Scott rescued a cadet from drowning would Ruger grant a reprieve to this future superintendent and army chief of staff.

Ruger's successor, John Schofield, proved to be one of hazing's toughest foes, though he had been known as the worst prankster in the Corps during his own cadet days in the early 1850s. He told cadet officers it was their duty to protect plebes from mistreatment. Failure to do so, he warned, would bring down upon them the same punishment imposed on hazers—trial by court-martial and dismissal. He also ruled that plebes who failed to report hazing were as guilty as those who abused them. He even took the unprecedented step of requiring drill masters "to properly regulate the tone and character of the voice in which commands and instructions are given; to avoid harsh, improper or even unnecessary words." Schofield felt so strongly that he addressed the entire Corps on the subject of hazing one summer day in 1879. "The discipline which makes the soldiers of a free country reliable in battle is not to be gained by harsh and tyrannical treatment," he declared. "On the contrary, such treatment is far more likely to defeat than to make an army." These words and others from that address have endured for many decades on a bronze plaque hanging in the barracks area and in the minds of generations of plebes required to memorize them.

Schofield, like other superintendents, felt sure he had successfully suppressed hazing, but it kept springing back with ever more sadistic embellishments. By 1900 the commandant of cadets, Colonel Otto I. Hein, was calling "the pernicious system of underground hazing" nothing less than "the root of all evil at the Military Academy."

Commandant Hein may well have had in mind the notorious case of Oscar Lyle Booz. Soon after Booz entered the Academy in June 1898, upperclassmen began to size him up as a perfect candidate for intense hazing. There was his unfortunate name, of course, along with his slight physical stature, bookish nature, sensitive demeanor, and lack of military bearing. One day on guard duty, he was intentionally given confusing and contradictory commands by older cadets. The plebe got all mixed up and marched and stood guard improperly. Third Classmen concluded he probably was not cut out to be an officer and decided to further test his mettle by calling Booz out for bareknuckled fisticuffs.

Above: *Major General John Schofield became superintendent of the Academy in 1876.* Below: *This pair of Colt Model 1861 Navy Revolvers were presented to Schofield by "his friends in St. Louis" while he commanded the Department of the Missouri.*

West Point Museum Collections, USMA

During the previous decade organized fistfights had become a prominent cadet arena associated with hazing. These matches were intended to toughen up plebes, weed out unfit ones, and discipline those who resisted hazing. They were organized by the so-called scrapping committee maintained by each of the upper classes. The committee designated the time and place, set the rules for two-minute rounds and one-minute rests, and provided the referee, timekeeper, and sentinels who kept watch to make certain no tactical officers happened upon the event. The committee also selected from its own class the plebe's opponent—someone of roughly the same height and weight but almost always an experienced fighter. An average of one fight a month was staged during this period—usually resulting in black eyes, bruised ribs, and broken jaws—and only one in ten was won by plebes. The Corps's frequent visitor,

Mark Twain, who disdained hazers as "bullies and cowards," nonetheless approved of the West Point fistfight: "I think it makes boys manly."

Oscar Booz's trial by fists took place on secluded high ground at Fort Putnam, near the site of the modern football stadium. His Third Class opponent, Frank Keller of Missouri, matched Booz in size but was far more muscular. Booz held his own in the first round but went down repeatedly in the next round. His seconds helped him get to his feet. Then he took a solid blow in the solar plexus, in the pit of the stomach. Booz collapsed, weeping and struggling for breath. After a few feeble attempts to rise, he fell back. Blood was streaming from his nose, and a cut under one eye was bleeding; the other eye was black, several teeth loose, and the area near his heart bruised. Booz gasped that he could fight no more. "You are a better man than I," he told his opponent. The rule was that a combatant had to keep fighting until he could not stand. The upper-class spectators were not satisfied that Booz was sufficiently beaten, and they taunted him as a coward. "I think they just wanted to kill me, if possible or come as near it as possible," Booz wrote his father the following day. "The fellows here are brutes, and they have evil in their minds."

USMA Archives

The death of Oscar Lyle Booz in 1900 prompted Congress to pass legislation to control hazing at West Point.

Instead of ending Booz's ordeal, the fight launched it in earnest. Older cadets began a systematic campaign of harassment. A favorite form of hazing was to force plebes to drink a bit of Tabasco sauce with every meal. Booz had to drink more than a bit, though just how much became a subject of debate. In any event, his throat grew so badly inflamed that he could drink little besides water. A month after classes began in September, Booz resigned and went home to Bristol, Pennsylvania. His spirit shattered and his health deteriorated, he died two years later of tuberculosis. On his deathbed, he hallucinated that he was still being hazed at West Point.

Reports of the former cadet's mistreatment at West Point set off a national scandal. His family charged that hazing had led to his death; the minister of Booz's Presbyterian church, preaching his funeral, said a "dangerous liquid"—the hot sauce—had triggered his downward spiral. The story, with its suggestion of sadism at a revered national institution, proved to be ideal grist for big-city newspapers whose sensational yellow journalism had recently helped spark the Spanish-American War. Less than a month after Booz's death, the secretary of war appointed a court of inquiry, including three general officers. Almost simultaneously, the U.S. House of Representatives named a five-man select committee to investigate the death and the larger issue of hazing at West Point.

Medical testimony during both investigations focused on the possible harm done by the repeated dosings of Tabasco sauce. Leading authorities on throat diseases were asked whether the hot sauce could have weakened the throat lining and allowed the tubercular

HAZING AT THE WEST POINT MILITARY ACADEMY

bacilli to flourish. No such medical link could be established, though the House committee's final report would allow for the "possibility" that hazing somehow hastened death.

Though neither inquiry found a connection between the hot sauce and Booz's death, the intense national focus on hazing threw the future of West Point into question. Several congressmen talked about the possibility of closing down the Academy. "The people are outraged by this practice," declared U.S. Senator Henry M. Teller of Colorado. "We have got to stop it, or eventually dismantle the institution." The threat seemed so real that the entire Corps took the extraordinary step of assembling on January 19, 1901, and agreeing to a statement to be presented to the House select committee by the four class presidents. The statement pledged "to discontinue hazing, the requiring of fourth class men to eat anything against their desire, and the practice of 'calling out' fourth class men."

Perhaps mollified by this pledge, Congress six weeks later approved mild legislation ordering the superintendent to devise regulations to prevent hazing. West Point had survived. So, too, in ameliorated form, had the practice that would bedevil new generations of first-year cadets.

This drawing of the fight between Frank Keller (on the right) and Oscar Booz appeared in a 1901 issue of Harper's Weekly. *Sketches of various hazing practices are shown around the border.*

USMA Archives

CHAPTER SIX

1902—1952

A NEW CENTURY

To help celebrate the completion of West Point's first century of existence, this bastion of military professionalism called upon the nation's best-known amateur soldier. The fact that the amateur in question—Theodore Roosevelt, recently commander of the famed Rough Riders—happened to be the president of the United States rendered the invitation all the more fitting. Roosevelt arrived by train on June 11, 1902, reviewed the Corps of Cadets, and mingled with veterans of the Long Gray Line who had served variously in the Mexican War, the Civil War, and the Spanish-American War.

At every turn during the elaborate round of speeches, parades, and dress balls, attended by ranking government officials, distinguished educators, and foreign diplomats, the president addressed praise to the Military Academy and its graduates. "This institution has completed its first hundred years of life," he declared. "During that century no other

West Point's centennial celebration attracted dignitaries from all over the globe.

Library of Congress

educational institution in the land has contributed as many names as West Point has contributed to the honor roll of the nation's greatest citizens."

Taking stock of that honor roll, West Point officials could proudly report that more than 10 percent of its 4,067 graduates during its first century had become general officers. Nearly 60 percent of its graduates had embraced second careers in civilian life.

There were entrepreneurs, industrialists and engineers, college presidents and railroad chief executives, bankers and lawyers, mayors, congressmen and U.S. senators—not to speak of one of Teddy Roosevelt's predecessors in the White House, Ulysses S. Grant. Only two years previously the names of precisely 5.6 percent of the Academy's living graduates had appeared in *Who's Who in America*, a proportion higher than any other American educational institution.

> " OF ALL THE INSTITUTIONS IN THIS COUNTRY NONE IS MORE ABSOLUTELY AMERICAN . . . THAN THIS. HERE WE CARE NOTHING FOR THE BOY'S BIRTHPLACE, NOR HIS CREED, NOR HIS SOCIAL STANDING; HERE WE CARE NOTHING SAVE FOR HIS WORTH AS HE IS ABLE TO SHOW IT."
>
> — PRESIDENT THEODORE ROOSEVELT

"And of all the institutions in this country," Roosevelt pointed out, "none is more absolutely American . . . more absolutely democratic than this. Here we care nothing for the boy's birthplace, nor his creed, nor his social standing; here we care nothing save for his worth as he is able to show it."

But in looking ahead to West Point's second century, Roosevelt saw the need to issue a caveat to the assembled cadets. Warfare was changing, he said, implying that the Academy would have to change with it. "I think it is going to be a great deal harder to be a first-class officer in the future than it has been in the past. In addition to the courage and steadfastness that have always been the prime requirements in a soldier, you have got to show far greater fertility of resource and far greater power of individual initiative than has ever been necessary."

He may have had in mind the difficulties recently experienced during the Spanish-American War. As commander of the First Volunteer Cavalry Regiment—the Rough Riders—he had seen firsthand the challenge of mobilizing an army for campaigning beyond America's borders. The invasion of Cuba had proved to be a logistical nightmare marked by rampant disease, inadequate rations, and obsolescent arms. In the new century, not the least because of Roosevelt's own policies, America would emerge from isolation and become a prominent player on the world stage. The need for a corps of professional officers prepared to train and lead citizen-soldiers in war would further challenge—and vindicate—Thomas Jefferson's original vision for West Point.

The most noticeable change at West Point over the next decade or so was in size. By 1916 the number of cadets authorized by Congress nearly tripled, to 1332. To keep pace, Congress approved the most ambitious construction program yet undertaken. It accounted for half a dozen new buildings: North Barracks, the administration building, the new Cadet Chapel, the East Gymnasium, the riding hall, and the East Academic Building. Native granite quarried for the construction from nearby hillsides enhanced the Academy's dominant architectural theme of massive gray Gothic.

The new chapel, completed in 1910 and overlooking the Plain, crowned the burst of building activity. Its organ, with more than twenty-two thousand pipes, is said to be the largest church organ in the world. Outside, the chapel set the architectural tone for the new structures, combining "the techniques and shapes of Gothic"—West Point literature would later make clear—"with the massiveness of medieval fortresses." At the urging of alumni, the old chapel it replaced was dismantled stone by stone and then reerected in the West Point Cemetery. Magazine articles focusing on the chapel and other construction trumpeted "the new West Point."

But defenders as well as critics conceded that "the old West Point" better characterized what was happening in the classroom. The curriculum and methods of teaching it changed scarcely at all. "West Point is not a subject for reform," wrote Hugh Scott, who became superintendent in 1906. "It goes forward on its majestic course from

The new Cadet Chapel, dedicated in 1910, replaced the Old Cadet Chapel, which was moved, stone by stone, and reconstructed at the edge of the West Point Cemetery.

© Ted Spiegel

"WEST POINT IS NOT A SUBJECT FOR
REFORM. IT GOES FORWARD ON ITS
MAJESTIC COURSE FROM YEAR TO
YEAR TOWARD THE FULFILLMENT
OF ITS DESTINY . . . IMPROVED FROM
TIME TO TIME TO KEEP IT ABREAST
OF THE AGE, BUT WITHOUT NEED
OF RADICAL ALTERATION."

— SUPERINTENDENT HUGH SCOTT

year to year toward the fulfillment of its destiny . . . improved from time to time to keep it abreast of the age, but without need of radical alteration."

Curriculum still focused on engineering and mathematics. French was taught, but grammar only—no conversation. All this perplexed the president, who had recently lavished such praise on the Academy at its centennial celebration. In 1908 Teddy Roosevelt wrote the secretary of war and future president, William Taft: "It seems to me a very great misfortune to lay so much stress upon mathematics in the curriculum at West Point and fail to have languages taught in accordance with the best conversational methods. I have several times called attention to it, but nothing had been done."

Rote learning ruled the classroom as it had since the days of Sylvanus Thayer nearly a century before. Professors handed each day's lesson to instructors, who then delivered it unchanged to each section with little explanation or room for discussion. Every cadet was expected to recite an approved answer to a standard question and then be graded on his performance. While reciting, the cadet typically stood at the blackboard with a pointer in hand. Precisely how he stood, even the angle at which he held the pointer, was prescribed by regulations. Anyone who attempted to update this system quickly encountered problems. In 1908 the

Academy took the unusual step of bringing in a civilian, John C. Adams of Yale, to head the new Department of English and History. Adams, to the consternation of his colleagues, dropped the use of instructors and taught all the classes himself. He lasted only two years before returning to Yale.

The study of military art and history remained locked in the past. Professors took little notice even in 1914 when an enormous new war began to engulf Europe. While the French army bled to death in front of the big guns of Verdun, West Point cadets memorized nineteenth-century cavalry tactics. This was a cause for wonder when General of the Army Omar N. Bradley looked back on his days as a member of the Class of 1915: "None of the new tactics or technology employed in Europe caused the slightest change in the curriculum at West Point. We continued to study men and campaigns of the Civil War for the most part and, as First Classmen, spent three days at Gettysburg, thoroughly grounding ourselves in that battle."

But the impact of World War I on West Point—and the Academy's effect on the war—surfaced with a jolt after America's entry in 1917. The two-million-man

Above: *Cadets demonstrate parts of speech in an English class, circa 1908.*

American Expeditionary Force to France was led by General John J. Pershing, Class of 1886. "His interest in detail is insatiable," newspaper correspondent Heywood Broun wrote of Pershing. "He can read a man's soul through his boots or his buttons." To organize the largest American army ever assembled under a single commander, Pershing depended upon his own old training. "The standards for the American army will be those of West Point," he ordered. "The rigid attention, the upright bearing, attention to detail, uncomplaining obedience to instruction required of the cadet will be required of every officer and soldier of our armies in France."

Pershing relied upon his old classmates and other West Point graduates to staff the high command as well. Three-quarters of American generals were products of the

Academy; thirty-four of thirty-eight corps and division commanders in France were West Pointers. They served, Pershing observed, "in the old West Point spirit." Secretary of War Newton D. Baker was happy to report, "West Point again demonstrated its supreme value to the country in the hour of need."

The desperate need for thousands of new company-grade officers in the burgeoning wartime army disrupted West Point, threatening to turn it into a glorified officer candidate school. The demands of war threw the orderly procession of classes into chaos. To begin with, the Class of 1917 graduated two months early. Members insisted upon this, as had the First Classmen at the beginning of the Civil War and Spanish-American War, in order to fill the choice positions in the army ahead of all the civilians being commissioned as so-called emergency officers. Under orders from the War Department, the Class of 1918 graduated ten months early; the Class of 1919 graduated a year early. On November 1, 1918, only ten days before the armistice, two additional classes graduated. Only the plebes remained on campus, scheduled under a War Department edict to graduate in June 1919.

Turmoil marked the postwar months. Three distinct and differently clad groups of students marched across the Plain. One group, the plebes remaining after the graduation

This 1918 oil painting by Raymond Desvarreux is titled "C. Clarke, Bugler, 15th NY Infantry." The 15th New York regiment was one of the first black regiments to reach France during World War I.

> ## " THE STANDARDS FOR THE AMERICAN ARMY WILL BE THOSE OF WEST POINT."
> — GENERAL JOHN J. PERSHING

of the two upper classes the previous November, wore the traditional cadet gray. The second group, formerly the Class of 1921, which had graduated in November, was clad in the olive-drab blouses of commissioned army officers; known as student officers, they returned to West Point for six months' of additional cadet training scarcely four weeks after graduation. Cadet-gray uniforms were unavailable for the third group, who had arrived in November. These cadets stood out in salvaged army private's uniforms with canvas leggings and campaign hats circled with orange bands. The distinctive hatbands inspired their nickname, the Orioles.

This jumbling of the customary class structure contributed to a growing disarray. The student officers lived separately from the rest of the corps and were even entitled to salutes from ordinary cadets and enlisted men. But they bridled under their treatment by the authorities, who insisted they be drilled and instructed as cadets. The normal four-year course of study had been shortened to one year during the war. After the war ended, however, Congress mandated a three-year course, embittering the group that had been promised graduation in June 1919 and now would not depart until 1921.

The administration consisted largely of older officers called back from retirement during the war. Despite the efforts of officers, hazing persisted from some upperclass cadets. One of its special targets, a new Oriole who wrote poetry in his spare time, committed suicide with his rifle. Investigations of the Academy turbulence by both Congress and the War Department appeared imminent. Once again, commentators were publicly questioning the need for West Point.

Above: *This postcard shows the West Point Cadet Regimental Staff circa 1922.* Below: *Accompanied by Superintendent Douglas MacArthur, General George Pershing reviews the graduating Class of 1920.*
USMA Archives

In the spring of 1919, the army's chief of staff, General Peyton C. March, decided to do something about the disarray on the Hudson. He wanted a new superintendent with the brilliance and boldness to straighten out the short-term mess and stop and reverse what he saw as the Academy's long-term decline. He summoned one of the army's brightest

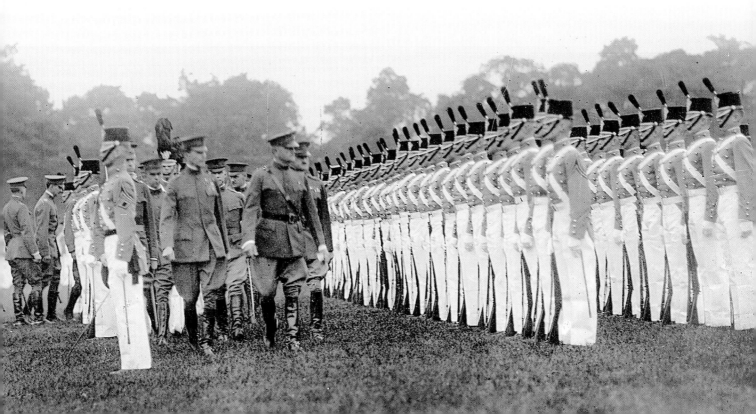

young stars, Brigadier General Douglas MacArthur, a brave division commander who had been one of the war's most highly decorated American officers. "The Military Academy is forty years behind the times," March told him. MacArthur protested, "I am not an educator. I am a field soldier." But March had made up his mind, and he ordered MacArthur, "Revitalize and revamp the Academy."

As a plebe, MacArthur had been singled out for hazing because his father, Arthur, was a brigadier general. It also probably did not help that at first he had something of a reputation as a mama's boy, because his mother lived at the West Point Hotel while his father was posted in the Philippines. In this he shared the fate of another military scion whose mother also lived in the hotel while her husband served in the Philippines—Ulysses S. Grant III, the grandson of the former general and president. But MacArthur soon proved himself an outstanding cadet. By his second year he was considered by a tactical officer "the finest drill master I have ever seen." MacArthur achieved the rare double distinction of being selected first captain of the Corps and graduating first in his Class of 1903.

When he took over as superintendent in June 1919, MacArthur was thirty-nine—the second youngest superintendent since Sylvanus Thayer, the revered father of the Academy, to whom he would sometimes be compared. MacArthur brought to his new post a studied informality of manner and appearance and an aura of aloofness. He brushed aside as superfluous the customary review of the Corps for the incoming superintendent. He shocked officers and cadets alike with his unconventional uniform. He wore old infantry puttees bound with straps curling with age and a battered, shapeless cap from which he had removed the wire stiffener. In cold weather he favored the short overcoat that had been forbidden by General Pershing during the war. He habitually carried a riding crop, which he would lift casually toward the peak

" I AM NOT AN EDUCATOR. I AM A FIELD SOLDIER. "

— B R I G A D I E R G E N E R A L
D O U G L A S M A C A R T H U R

Douglas MacArthur, pictured with his mother, during his first year at West Point.

of his cap to acknowledge salutes. He strode with a majestic bearing, aloof from other officers as well as the Corps of Cadets. "Neither I nor the vast majority of my class ever saw the general," wrote W. S. Nye, "except when he was walking across [the] diagonal walk, apparently lost in thought, his nose in the air, gazing at distant horizons as his publicity photos always portrayed him throughout his career."

One of MacArthur's great admirers, William A. Ganoe, the West Point adjutant, thought him "a complete contradiction"—both "a patrician and a plebeian." This paradox is illustrated in a tale of uncertain veracity that has appeared in various forms over the years. Still a bachelor, MacArthur liked to give the appearance of living a Spartan existence in the superintendent's imposing house with its staff of servants and such elegant accoutrements as gold dinner plates. On one occasion, hosting a group of New York sportswriters at lunch, he escorted his guests to the basement and showed them the simple cot

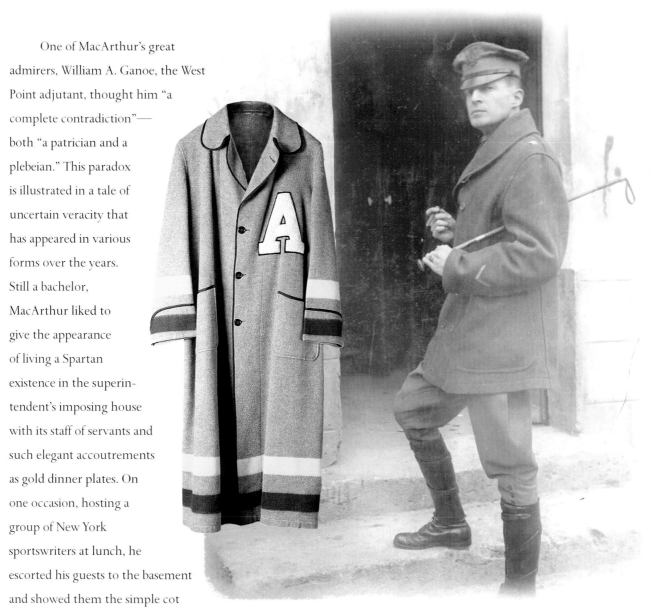

where he said he often slept. Later, after the cook reported one of the gold plates missing, MacArthur wrote the sportswriters asking about it. One of them replied that if the superintendent slept in the basement as often as he had said, he would have found the missing plate where the writer had hidden it—between the two blankets piled on the cot.

MacArthur set out to impose a new vision on the Academy. During the war, while leading patrols in the no-man's-land beyond the trenches of France armed with no more than a swagger stick, he had learned the army's need for a different kind of officer. Modern armies, he realized, would consist of a new breed of citizen-soldiers, who had to be led through understanding and respect rather than fear and strict regimentation. West Point therefore must "deliver a product trained with a view to teaching, leading, and inspiring the modern citizen." The new officer, he believed, would be "a type possessing all the cardinal military virtues as of yore, but possessing an intimate understanding of his fellows, a comprehensive grasp of world and national affairs."

Above: *During his time as superintendent, MacArthur was almost always seen with his trademark riding crop.*
USMA Archives

Inset: *MacArthur's cadet bathrobe carries the letter "A," which he received as a member of the 1901—02 varsity baseball team.*
West Point Museum Collections, USMA

High among the new superintendent's priorities was breaking down the traditional isolation that left cadets, in his words, "cloistered almost to a monastic extent." He persuaded the English department to require the reading of two newspapers daily and the

MacArthur advocated the reading of two newspapers daily in order to keep in touch with current events.

discussion of the day's events during the first ten minutes of class. He brought in scholars, political leaders, and military experts to address the Corps. One of the most electrifying and prescient lectures was delivered by Brigadier General William Mitchell on the future of air power.

At the same time, cadets were encouraged to experience the larger world on their own. Previously the only time cadets could leave the post was for summer furlough at the end of the third year. MacArthur granted upperclassmen six-hour leaves on weekends and two-day furloughs during the summer. For the first time, moreover, they were allowed to handle cash; they received five dollars of their monthly pay of fifty dollars to spend as they pleased. First Classmen were permitted to fraternize with post officers, visit their homes, even play cards with them and their wives.

A tactical noncommissioned officer helps shepherd new cadets through "Beast Barracks" exercises.

All cadets were required to learn how to waltz and two-step under the tutelage of a professional dancing instructor. Their partners were faculty wives and daughters. On weekends, the cadets' dates— young flappers in cloche hats— descended upon august Cullum Hall to demonstrate such dance crazes of the day as the camel walk and the toddle.

MacArthur also loosened a bit the straitjacket of petty rules. He allowed cadets to smoke cigarettes in their rooms, a practice that had been carried on surreptitiously for many years. The liberalized policy sometimes had a salutory effect. "That took the fun out of the game," recalled Maxwell D. Taylor, Class of 1922. "I never smoked thereafter and remain today a nonsmoker, thanks to Douglas MacArthur."

The new superintendent's liberalization of regulations upset alumni and professors alike. By allowing more freedom, they feared, he would undermine the bedrock of order and discipline upon which the Academy rested. Even more shocking was MacArthur's decision to abolish the traditional summer encampment at Fort Clinton, just east of Trophy Point. This represented one of the Academy's oldest and most hallowed traditions. For more than a century, cadets had lived there under canvas for two months, doing a bit of drill and tactical training in the morning, lounging about in the afternoon, eating good food served by civilian waiters in a palatial mess hall and attending concerts and dress balls in the evening.

MacArthur saw it as "a ludicrous caricature of life in the field." He asked rhetorically, "How long are we going on preparing for the War of 1812?" He answered his question by ending the practice and ordering cadets in the First and Third Classes to Camp Dix, New Jersey, where they trained with regular army troops with modern weapons and tactics developed during the recent war. Afterward, they marched back to West Point carrying full combat gear. Such was the outcry from alumni and from officers and wives deprived of their summer social season that after two years of trying authentic training at Camp Dix, MacArthur's successor, Superintendent Fred Sladen, reinstated the old summer encampment, which would continue until 1942 and World War II.

*Cadets socialize at
Summer Camp in 1881.*

USMA Archives

A far more enduring innovation was the new athletic program MacArthur created.
He had a passion for sports. One of his "happiest memories" as a cadet, he wrote later, was
scoring the winning run in the first Army-Navy baseball game, in 1901. As superintendent
he haunted baseball and football practice, passing on tips to the coaches and players. Earl
Blaik, star of the Army football team and later its longtime coach, recalled, "Never a

practice period passed that did not see the Supe, carrying a riding crop, jauntily striding on the practice field." MacArthur once tried without success to show Blaik, who was also a mainstay on the basketball and baseball teams, how to hit a curveball. "It must have been the only time I ever saw him fail to accomplish something he set out to do." In fact, among MacArthur's failures as superintendent was his inability to persuade the U.S. Congress to build a fifty-thousand-seat football stadium equipped with elaborate rail yards to accommodate special trains for spectators.

But in intramural athletics MacArthur made his mark. Though West Point maintained a vigorous physical fitness program under Herman Koehler, the master of the sword, MacArthur saw room for expansion. MacArthur's war experiences had persuaded him that "the men who had taken part in organized sports made the best soldiers." He sold Koehler on intramural team sports and enlisted the aid of the chaplain, Clayton Wheat, an enthusiastic sports fan who supported staging competitive events on Sunday afternoons, which previously had been sacrosanct. Under the slogan "Every cadet an athlete," MacArthur required every company to field a team in nine different sports: football, baseball, soccer, lacrosse, tennis, basketball, track and field, golf, and polo. Every cadet

USMA Archives

West Point Museum
Collections, USMA

HOW THE
BIG GAME
BEGAN

Dennis Mahan Michie (pronounced my-key) was a high-spirited cadet who loved the sport of football, which he had played in prep school. In 1890 he organized a team and coached it himself. To generate enthusiasm, he arranged for some midshipman friends at the Naval Academy to issue a challenge for a game. He then took the challenge to his influential father, Professor Peter Smith Michie, head of the Academic Board, and persuaded him to agree to the game, which was scheduled for the end of the season.

Young Michie and his players trained by rising half an hour before reveille and jogging around the Plain. The superintendent allowed them to practice only on those Saturday afternoons when rain prevented the usual dress parade. They had to buy their own uniforms: white-laced canvas jackets and white breeches, black woolen stockings, and cap. "What they don't know about the game would fill an encyclopedia," observed a veteran player from Yale who came down to offer advice, "but they have the right type of men for it."

The first Army-Navy game was played on November 29, 1890, on the southeast corner of the parade ground. About a thousand spectators attended, many of them members of the Corps of Cadets, who had financed the opponent's travel expenses by paying fifty-two cents apiece. They were treated to a bruising battle, but Navy, which had been playing football for eight years, did most of the bruising. Midshipmen surprised Army players by calling out nautical commands for plays—"splice the main brace" for a plunge over center; "tack ship" for a halfback sweep around the right end. Army coach and captain Dennis Michie retaliated with his own improvised commands, "in battery, heave" and "left wheel." Navy stunned everyone by faking a punt and then running for a touchdown. The trick play brought indignant protests from West Point fans that such conduct was ungentlemanly. Navy won, 24–0, and went on to capture two out of the next three games.

The annual game excited so much interest that a near riot erupted in New York's Army-Navy Club in 1893. "The excitement attending it exceeds all reasonable limit," said Superintendent Oswald Ernst in recommending suspension of the series. After a hiatus of six years, the rivalry was resumed in 1899 and interrupted again only three more times, including during World War I. The cadet responsible for one of the most celebrated rivalries in college sports, Dennis Michie, did not live to see the resumption of the series. He was killed in the Spanish-American War at San Juan Hill in Cuba in 1898. West Point's Michie Stadium, dedicated in 1924, honors his memory.

Counter-clockwise from top left: The first *Army-Navy football game; a West Point football jersey circa 1900; Michie Stadium; cadet fans sport "Beat Navy" paraphernalia.*

© Ted Spiegel

had to participate in at least one of these endeavors. The contests turned out to be so spirited, especially in football and lacrosse, that the intramural program was soon dubbed "intra-murder." On the stone portals of the gymnasium, MacArthur had inscribed a testament to sports that he personally composed:

> *Upon the fields of friendly strife*
> *Are sown the seeds*
> *That, upon other fields, on other days,*
> *Will bear the fruits of victory*

Another enduring contribution during the MacArthur years gave formal structure to the traditional honor system. The origins of the honor code dated back a century to even before Thayer and his insistence on truth telling. From time to time ad hoc vigilance committees had been selected by the cadets to consider honor violations, but they lacked official sanction. In 1922 MacArthur, knowing from combat that "success or failure . . . may depend upon an officer's word," created an Honor Committee to administer the code. The committee, comprised of representatives selected by the cadets from each company, had no punitive power but served as a kind of grand jury to call attention to breaches of the honor code. The honor system thus became one of the few significant aspects of cadet life that was administered largely by the cadets themselves.

Like many of his predecessors, MacArthur had to wrestle with the practice of hazing. Eliminating it was one of his primary goals. He remembered not only his own experience as a plebe but also the stories he had heard in France. "There were officers overseas shot in the back by their own men," he said, "simply because they had been brought up with the mistaken idea that bullying was leadership." But like other superintendents who tried to abolish physical and mental abuse, he ran into resistance from cadets and from alumni—some of whom wrote letters, reported the adjutant, "denouncing the supe as the wrecker of West Point."

In the hazing controversy, as in other matters, MacArthur's grand vision was accompanied by a thin skin. Soon after taking over, he had been persuaded to allow the cadets to publish a weekly newspaper. It seemed to fit nicely with his idea of opening up the Academy. But when opposition to his hazing reforms appeared in the newspaper—he was accused of making the plebe year "a bed of roses"—he had every available copy confiscated and burned. The officer in charge received a new assignment, far from West Point.

The cadet Honor Committee, shown here in the 1924 Howitzer, was established by Douglas MacArthur in 1922 to provide structure to the Academy's honor system.

SCHMIDT   CUMMINGS   BLANCHARD   DANIEL
SKINNER   MOORE, L.S.   JOHN   MAGLIN   MOORE, C.E.
HILL, D.C.   HILL, J.G.   O'NEILL   LEE, R.V.

Honor Committee

PACH BRO'S   841 B'WAY, N.Y.

USMA Archives

MacArthur at length gathered a small group of First Classmen and plied them with cigarettes and personal charm. At his request they formed a committee and prepared a pamphlet on hazing. The pamphlet listed certain "unacceptable" treatment of plebes such as prearranged fistfights or performing splits over a bayonet. The reforms did not go far enough to suit MacArthur; the pamphlet, after all, listed "acceptable" hazing. At the suggestion of the commandant of cadets, his old friend Robert M. Danford, MacArthur struck at the heart of hazing by eliminating the introductory ritual where it flourished—Beast Barracks. Instead of upperclassmen, tactical officers would shepherd plebes through their three-week orientation.

Opposite: *Officers' quarters at West Point; in the distance is Buffalo Soldier Field.*

© Ted Spiegel

MacArthur's greatest challenge came in his attempts to modernize the curriculum. This was the province of the thirteen-member Academic Board, which consisted of department heads, the commandant, and the superintendent. Most of the members of the board were old-timers; five had been professors when MacArthur had been a mere plebe, more than a score of years earlier. MacArthur could count on only three votes—his own vote, Commandant Danford's, and that of Lucius H. Holt, a Yale Ph.D. with no previous military experience who had headed the Department of English and History since 1910. One of the few issues all could agree on was the importance of resuming the customary four-year course of study, which Congress approved in 1920.

Most of the professors opposed practically all of MacArthur's other proposals. They saw him as a transient, another "boy superintendent" who would soon move on; MacArthur viewed them as entrenched guardians of the past. "The professors are so secure," he told his adjutant, "they have become set and smug. They deliver the same schedule year after year with the blessed unction that they have reached the zenith in education." The

Above: *Cadets attend a lecture circa 1904.*

USMA Archives

majority of the board simply did not share his vision of the need for a new type of versatile officer capable of leading citizen-soldiers. "The Military Academy," said the board in its own 1920 report, "is intended to impart a specialized training for a specialized purpose."

Achieving change on the board was a process that required gradually building consensus by wooing its conservative members. MacArthur felt he lacked the time; he was transient, the board permanent. Certainly he lacked the patience and the tact—as indeed did several of the professors. At one meeting he started to describe in detail his proposal to bring in as instructors regular army officers who had graduated from civilian institutions instead of West Point. A professor began to interrupt his presentation and grew so intrusive that MacArthur exploded. He banged his fist on the table and commanded, "Sit down, sir. I am the superintendent!" A hush descended on the room, and he added, "Even if I weren't, I should be treated in a gentlemanly manner."

MacArthur further alienated the professors by trespassing on their sanctuaries as no superintendent had ever dared. He visited the professors in their offices and paid periodic visits to classes. He would suddenly appear in the classroom, take a seat in the rear, and afterward suggest ways professors and instructors could improve teaching methods. He especially encouraged instructors to conduct less routine recitation and more lectures and discussions. The professors thought such a proposal "a dangerous innovation." Looking back later, Roger H. Nye, a professor of history at West Point, concluded, "By the summer of 1921, MacArthur had so completely drained the faculty and alumni of good will that he could no longer innovate, and was instead waging a defense of all that he had changed."

> " ON THE ASHES OF OLD WEST POINT,
> I HAVE BUILT A NEW WEST POINT—
> STRONG, VIRILE AND ENDURING. "
>
> — SUPERINTENDENT DOUGLAS
> MACARTHUR

The academic program at West Point has evolved in response to the needs of the army and trends in higher education. Most academic courses are taught much the same as they are at civilian institutions, though class size is much smaller.

© Ted Spiegel

He won only incremental changes. Officers recalled to serve as instructors at West Point now spent their first year taking refresher courses at civilian universities. Each professor would visit at least three other campuses a year to observe and absorb new ideas and methods. History and English were divided into two departments. MacArthur asked for new courses in the social sciences intended to broaden a cadet's horizons but got only one course, which combined economics and political science. Cadets in natural philosophy could now use a slide rule; chemistry added a lesson in the internal combustion engine; military art and history substituted the battles of World War I for the campaigns of the Civil War. "The success obtained" in curriculum, MacArthur admitted, "did not even approximate to what I had in mind."

The Hotel Thayer, a West Point landmark since 1926, commands a spectacular view of the Hudson River.
© Ted Spiegel

MacArthur expected to remain at least four years, like many of his predecessors. But his tenure was cut short in 1922 by reassign-ment to the Philippines. The army chief of staff, Jack Pershing, explained that MacArthur's name had simply risen to the top of a roster of general officers available for foreign service. But MacArthur's reforms were generating controversy in Washington as well as West Point. His biographer, D. Clayton James, suggested that the foreign duty rationale "served as a convenient pretext for removing a refractory individualist who created difficulties and embarrassments for the War Department." MacArthur offered no protest and in fact felt great pride in what he had accomplished in three years. "On the ashes of Old West Point," he proclaimed, "I have built a New West Point—strong, virile and enduring."

Though his immediate successor restored the summer encampment to its Napoleonic splendor, brought back the old Beast Barracks, and otherwise did his best to reverse the MacArthur reforms, the seeds of change had taken root. The willingness to experiment and break with tradition could not be snuffed out, and future superintendents revived MacArthur's spirit of questioning everything. "Slowly his innovations would be restored, his ideas accepted," wrote the historian Stephen Ambrose. "If Sylvanus Thayer dominated West Point in the nineteenth century, Douglas MacArthur dominated it in the twentieth.

The Cadet Mess in the early 1900s (above) and today (below). The entire Corps of Cadets eats breakfast and lunch at the same time in less than twenty-five minutes.

The chief difference was that Thayer had sixteen years in which to impose his personality and ideas, while MacArthur had but three."

MacArthur's thwarted aim to expand the social sciences curriculum was carried out by a soldier-scholar who came to typify the faculty of the new generation. Herman Beukema, Class of 1915, who succeeded Holt as head of the Department of Economics, Government, and History, introduced a series of new courses that broadened the horizons of the cadets. In 1934 he launched a full course on international relations. In 1938 he expanded a course on U.S. government to compare the governments of the major world powers. In 1940 he introduced a course with the timely name Economics of War. Beukema was preparing cadets intellectually for a new kind of war. One of the many lecturers he brought to the post, Sir Alfred Zimmern of Oxford University, remarked after his address in 1938: "I have seldom, if ever, encountered a group of students who struck me as having been better disciplined intellectually for the study of international relations. I had not expected to find in a military institution such intellectual keenness, such an open-minded and critical interest in problems lying outside what used to be considered . . . the sphere of the professional soldier."

"STUBBORN ENOUGH"
TO WIN FOUR STARS

He seemed ideal officer material. He was exceptionally bright, had taken courses at three universities, and was in excellent physical condition. His father was a veteran army officer who had instilled in him the virtues of hard work, self-discipline, and self-respect. But Benjamin O. Davis Jr. was black, and no African American had graduated from West Point in nearly half a century. Only two had been admitted, and neither survived more than six months.

Davis entered the Academy in 1932 after nomination by Illinois Representative Oscar De Priest, the only black member of Congress. Despite the passage of time, Davis received much the same treatment as had Henry O. Flipper and the other black pioneers at the Academy during the nineteenth century. He roomed alone and was subjected to social ostracism. "I was silenced solely because cadets did not want blacks at West Point," he wrote. "Their only purpose was to freeze me out. What they did not realize was that I was stubborn enough to put up with their treatment to reach the goal I had come to attain."

He graduated in 1936 in the top 15 percent of his class—35th of 276. He wanted to be a pilot, a dream born as a teenager when he had flown in a barnstorming airplane. The new Army Air Corps rejected his application. The rationale was that it had no black units, and long-standing army policy dictated that an African American could not command white troops. Instead, Davis was commissioned into the infantry as an officer in a black regiment.

Clockwise from above: Benjamin O. Davis Jr. and Congressman Oscar de Priest at Davis' graduation from West Point; Davis at the Tuskegee Institute in 1942; Davis is presented the stars of a brigadier general by General Earle E. Partridge.

But mobilization for World War II opened up new opportunities for African Americans. His father, Benjamin O. Davis Sr., who had enlisted in a black cavalry regiment in 1899, became the first African American to rise to brigadier general. A black fighter squadron was created by order of President Franklin D. Roosevelt, and young Davis was assigned to train with it at Tuskegee Institute in Alabama and become its commander. His 99th Fighter Squadron served with distinction during the war in North Africa, Sicily, and Italy. Then, based in Italy, his 332nd Fighter Group, with its four squadrons of Tuskegee airmen, escorted bombers on raids in Italy, Germany, and Eastern Europe. Not a single bomber escorted by the Tuskegee airmen was lost to an enemy fighter—a record unmatched by any unit with as many missions.

Davis later commanded racially integrated combat flying units in Korea and Vietnam. In 1965 he became the first African American in any military service to reach the rank of lieutenant general. In 1999, in retirement, he received the rare distinction of a fourth star—the final reward for the "pure obstinacy" that he said had governed his struggle against extraordinary odds.

When World War II came, West Point was much better prepared to cope with the challenge of total war than it had been in 1917. As faculty were called away, they were replaced by outstanding scholars and retired officers who were nongraduates—so many of them that they eventually comprised more than two-thirds of the officers on post. In 1942, by presidential directive, the course of study was reduced to three years for the duration, precluding the World War I chaos of cadets graduating after just one year of training. Better still, by introducing new training programs, the Academy avoided proposals that it be closed for the duration and converted into an officer training school. During the war Congress expanded the authorized size of the Corps to 2,496 cadets.

The purchase of more than ten thousand acres of nearby land permitted extensive tactical training of cadets. This new terrain featured such realistic facilities as concrete pillboxes, a mock freight train, moving target ranges, pontoon bridges, and a two-hundred-yard-long assault course. Beast Barracks was eliminated, and plebes spent their first summer receiving essentially the same basic training as draftees. Third Classmen devoted their summers to training at regular army bases. All cadets participated in full-scale maneuvers, usually with army divisions.

The most extraordinary change was the introduction of pilot training. Since 1936 cadets had been

Below: Cadets (circa 1900) raise and lower targets so other cadets can practice their rifle marksmanship.

USMA Archives

Bottom: Cadets (circa 2001) practice on an assault course.

© Ted Spiegel

receiving twenty hours of so-called air experience at various airfields. But in 1942 actual flight training began, first at civilian facilities and then at the Academy's newly acquired Stewart Field near Newburgh, New York. Those who chose to become air cadets constituted about 40 percent of the Corps. They underwent 257 hours of ground instruction, 402 hours in simulators such as the Link Trainer, and 205 hours in the air. More than a thousand cadets received their wings at graduation during the four years of the program beginning in 1943, receiving commissions in the Army Air Corps.

Above: *Hat and shoes worn by Joseph W. Stilwell, Class of 1904, as commander of American forces in the China-Burma-India Theater in 1942.*

West Point Museum Collections, USMA

As in previous wars, West Point alumni dominated the leadership of the World War II army. On a larger scale than ever, they met Thomas Jefferson's old challenge of being officers capable of transforming civilians into efficient and well-trained soldiers. Of the 155 commanders of units of division size and larger, 89 were Academy graduates. That this was a smaller percentage than in World War I could be accounted for by the number of nongraduates (those who were commissioned through ROTC or OCS) who had learned their trade well at the army's War College and other postgraduate schools. Four of the five generals who ascended to five-star rank—MacArthur, Omar Bradley,

Below: *A stuffed Army mule signed by World War II leaders, including Patton and Eisenhower.*

Dwight Eisenhower, and Henry "Hap" Arnold— were West Pointers. The fifth, Army Chief of Staff George Marshall, was a graduate of Virginia Military Institute, a school—Academy alumni were quick to point out—founded by a West Pointer upon West Point principles.

The West Pointers at the top during the war were a diverse lot. Their lives and records at the Academy often had little in common other

West Point Museum Collections, USMA

On the plaque:

"I WANT AN OFFICER FOR
A SECRET AND DANGEROUS
MISSION.
I WANT A WEST POINT
FOOTBALL PLAYER."
GENERAL GEORGE C. MARSHALL
CHIEF OF STAFF, U.S. ARMY—WORLD WAR II

By tradition, Army football players touch this plaque as they run onto the field at Michie Stadium.

© Ted Spiegel

than a mutual interest in athletics. Interestingly, one postwar study of Academy graduates found a "high positive relationship between participation in athletics and display of leadership traits as cadets and future success in the Army." Organized athletics, with their emphasis on competition and teamwork, were perhaps one clue to the continuing mystery of what personal characteristics and training make a great officer. "The business of producing soldiers is almost as arcane as running a seminary," the historian Thomas Fleming has suggested. "Ultimately, in both professions, the nonintellectual components of the personality are the decisive factors in success or failure."

As a cadet, Hap Arnold gave scarcely the slightest hint of the future hard-driving apostle of air power. The future commander of the Army Air Corps and later the U.S. Air Force recalled that he "skated along without too much effort in a spot just below the middle of the class." He played on the polo squad and as a substitute fullback in football. His classmates remembered him best for the Black Hand, the secret society he helped found to play boyish pranks. Arnold and the Black were responsible for such memorable mischief as hauling the reveille cannon onto the roof of the barracks. One night two months before graduation, he coordinated a massive fireworks show with a spectacular climax. Arnold mounted the barracks roof and ignited an elaborate pinwheel display—his body "silhouetted against the light of my own handiwork, in full view of the entire Corps." After several weeks of solitary confinement and walking endless punishment tours, Arnold was allowed to graduate in 1907. He desperately wanted the cavalry but was commissioned in the infantry. He

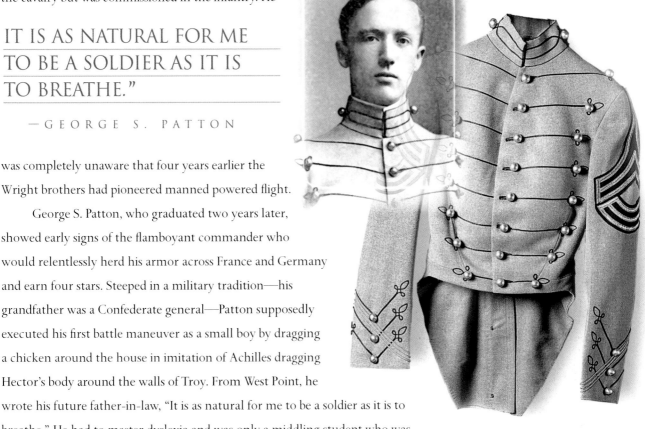

" ## IT IS AS NATURAL FOR ME TO BE A SOLDIER AS IT IS TO BREATHE."

— G E O R G E   S .   P A T T O N

was completely unaware that four years earlier the Wright brothers had pioneered manned powered flight.

George S. Patton, who graduated two years later, showed early signs of the flamboyant commander who would relentlessly herd his armor across France and Germany and earn four stars. Steeped in a military tradition—his grandfather was a Confederate general—Patton supposedly executed his first battle maneuver as a small boy by dragging a chicken around the house in imitation of Achilles dragging Hector's body around the walls of Troy. From West Point, he wrote his future father-in-law, "It is as natural for me to be a soldier as it is to breathe." He had to master dyslexia and was only a middling student who was turned back for a year. But he cultivated a meticulous appearance and soldierly bearing, achieving the high rank of adjutant his final year. He tried football (breaking both arms), ran the hurdles, and once tested his courage by suddenly standing erect on the rifle range while bullets whizzed by his head. Three decades later, when his son was nominated for the Academy, Patton advised him, "Do your damndest in an ostentatious manner all the time."

Omar Bradley and Dwight Eisenhower turned out to be the most illustrious members of the Class of 1915, though it was not immediately evident. This was the fabled "Class the Stars Fell On." Of the 164 graduates, 59 became general officers, collecting a total of 111 stars. Three wore four stars; two—Bradley and Ike—won five stars, and after the war each served as army chief of staff. At West Point, Bradley recalled, he "became almost obsessively absorbed in athletics." He played substitute center in football, and as a left-fielder demonstrated one of the finest throwing arms of any outfielder in Academy baseball history. From sports he learned "the important art of group cooperation in goal

The 1909 graduation photo and full-dress coat of Cadet Sergeant Major George S. Patton.

West Point Museum
Collections, USMA

achievement. No extracurricular endeavor I know of could better prepare a soldier for the battlefield." He graduated forty-fourth in the class and lived up to the quotation his friend Ike dug up and included in his yearbook portrait of the man who would serve as his right hand during World War II: "True merit is like a river, the deeper it is, the less noise it makes."

Eisenhower himself chose West Point for the free education and the opportunity to excel in sports. He later confessed to "a lack of motivation in almost everything other than athletics." Dubbed "one of the most promising backs in Eastern football," by the *New York Times*, he twisted his right knee in a game and then smashed it in a horseback-riding drill, ending his athletic career. After that, Eisenhower wrote, "Life seemed to have little meaning. A need to excel was gone." He began smoking, took up poker, and watched his grades fall. He was so depressed that classmates had to talk him out of handing in his resignation papers, and the ruined knee almost prevented him from receiving a commission.

But Ike proved to be as resilient as his trademark grin. He demonstrated his energy and enthusiasm as a cheerleader for the varsity football team and his organizational skills as coach of the junior varsity. Classmates loved his sense of humor. As a plebe, he and a classmate defied hazing by reporting for an after-hours inspection in full-dress coats, cross belts, and brass—but no trousers. An indifferent student who graduated 61st, he accumulated so many demerits that he ranked 125th in conduct. "I never could wear my hat straight, and I couldn't be bothered with dust in the corner of my room."

Nonetheless, a prescient tactical officer commented that Eisenhower "was born to command." And he did: supreme Allied commander in Europe, army chief of staff, commander of North Atlantic Treaty Organization forces in Europe, president of Columbia University, and thirty-fourth president of the United States. He was the second West Point graduate to be elected president, after that earlier indifferent cadet who went on to excel in war, Ulysses S. Grant. Except in their contrasting performances as chief executive—historians deemed Ike a success, Grant a failure—the two men followed paths that were remarkably parallel. Both came from homes of modest means in the American heartland, suffered through dispiriting times at West Point, displayed an unaffected manner that endeared them to classmates, graduated near the middle of the class, led the army to success in decisive wars, and served full terms as president.

Eisenhower needed time before he grasped the value of his days at West Point. For decades after graduation it appeared that the only lasting mark he had left beside the

Above: *Cadet Dwight D. Eisenhower's 1915 graduation photo.* Below: *General Eisenhower's coat and cap.*
USMA Archives

West Point Museum
Collections, USMA

Hudson was his name, which he had inscribed (IKE EISENHOWER, MAY 1914) on copper cladding atop the 145-foot high northern tower of the new chapel. Ironically it was in the army's new postgraduate schools, such as Command and General Staff School, that he began to demonstrate his leadership skills.

But he took an increasing interest in the Academy. Toward the end of his life, he observed, "West Point and all it means is so deep inside you that you are not so articulate about it. West Point did more for me than any other institution." He showed enormous pride when his son John received an appointment to the Academy in 1940 and great disappointment when he had to miss John's graduation because it occurred on June 6, 1944—that momentous D-Day in Europe—when the supreme Allied commander was otherwise engaged. As army chief of staff after the war, Eisenhower recommended that the Academy establish its first course in applied psychology as a way to help "improve leadership and personnel handling in the Army at large." Later, he eloquently summed up his own view of the Academy experience, "West Point gives its graduates something that far transcends the techniques and knowledge involved in developing, training and leading an Army. It helps them build character."

Eisenhower Hall serves as the Cadet Activities Center or student union. It contains a forty-five-hundred-seat auditorium, snack bar, and cafeteria.

© Ted Spiegel

Yet none of the great generals of World War II identified more with the Academy than the controversial former "supe" who had set it upon the path of modernization. Douglas MacArthur went on to lead U.S. forces to victory in the Pacific, preside over the birth of a democratic Japan, and, until his unfortunate break with President Harry Truman, command United Nations forces in the Korean War. In 1962, two years before his death, he returned to West Point to receive its highest honor, the Sylvanus Thayer Award, and to bid farewell. The old soldier concluded:

> "In my dreams, I hear again the crash of guns, the rattle of musketry, the
> strange mournful mutter of the battlefield.
>
> But in the evening of my memory, always I come back to West Point. Always
> there echoes and re-echoes Duty—Honor—Country.
>
> Today marks my final roll call with you. But I want you to know that when I
> cross the river my last conscious thoughts will be of The Corps, and The
> Corps, and The Corps."

En route to Ring Day ceremonies at Trophy Point, cadets in "India whites" pass the statue of General Douglas MacArthur and a stone wall bearing the West Point motto "Duty, Honor, Country."

© Ted Spiegel

1952—Present

CHALLENGE and RENEWAL

Major General William C. Westmoreland

liked to quip that he had one clear mandate from the White House when he assumed the post of superintendent in 1960. He said the only instruction he had received from that old alum, President Dwight Eisenhower, was, "Do something about that damned football team." Complying with Ike's desire to get Army back on the winning track, Westmoreland caused something of an uproar by hiring away the prestigious coach of Louisiana State University, Paul Dietzel. "It is to the national interest," he explained, "that we, by our performance, create the image of a winner."

The new superintendent had other ideas for creating "the image of a winner." Only forty-six years old when he took over at West Point, he stood ramrod straight as one of the army's fastest-rising stars. He had been first captain in the Class of 1936, made general at age thirty-eight (the youngest brigadier general in the army at that time), and now had a reputation as a hard charger who could do no wrong—a "water walker," in the soldiers' slang. His most ambitious goal at West Point was to substantially increase the size of the Corps of Cadets—from twenty-four hundred to forty-four hundred—to match the strength of the Brigade of Midshipmen at the Naval Academy.

Football provided a wedge for some high-level lobbying. "As I prepared to get the expansion bill started in the long trek through the bureaucracy," Westmoreland recalled, "a discussion with President Kennedy at the Army-Navy football game in December 1962 gave me an opportunity to make my point in person to the Commander in Chief."

Navy was headed toward a lopsided victory when the president turned to Westmoreland and asked, "General, why are there so many more midshipmen at the

General William Westmoreland, Class of 1936, became superintendent in 1960.
USMA Archives

153

GETTING THE NAVY'S GOAT

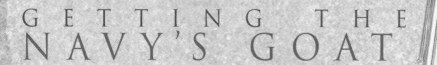

E very class has its merry mischief makers. In the Class of 1966, which would sustain heavy casualties in Vietnam, two of the leading pranksters were Tom Carhart and Art Mosley. During the weeks before the Army-Navy game of 1965, the pair directed their efforts at boosting morale at West Point, which had lost five out of the last six games with its service rivals. They purchased a thousand pairs of women's panties and a little printing press. On the panty bottoms they printed BEAT NAVY and sold them at five dollars a pair.

Then the two cadets came up with a more daring scheme. They would kidnap the Navy mascot, a goat named Billy XV. The weekend before the big game, they and half a dozen co-conspirators drove to Maryland. There they learned that security-conscious authorities at Annapolis had moved Billy from the Naval Academy dairy farm to an Atlantic Fleet communications center across the Severn River. The goat was secured in a pen topped with barbed wire inside a larger enclosure surrounded by a ten-foot fence with two marines guarding the gate.

The cadets, wearing black turtlenecks and with their faces darkened with burned cork, entered the compound through an unlocked pedestrian gate. While four young women they had enlisted as accomplices drove up to the main gate and flirted with the marine guards, the cadets dashed to the goat pen. They broke open the padlock with a crowbar wrapped in a black towel and made off with Billy, who curled up comfortably in a bed of straw in the rear of a cadet car.

Back at West Point, after the goat was safely stashed in the barn of Carhart's grandmother, the conspirators quickly spread the news via a mimeograph machine. When the superintendent stood on the poop deck of Washington Hall to make an announcement at the noon meal, the Corps responded by chanting, "We want the goat! We want the goat!"

Under intense pressure from the Pentagon, the goat was returned to the Navy. Carhart, Mosley, and the other culprits were hauled before West Point's commandant. "We've got to give you some punishment," he told them, "so I'm going to remove your first-class privileges for two months. But I want you to know I'd be proud to have you serve under me in the Army. Well done."

It took twenty-six years for the Navy to get even. In 1991 midshipmen mounted a midnight expedition to West Point. They kidnapped the army's prized mule mascots and showcased them in Annapolis forty-eight hours before the game. Commandants from the two institutions eventually signed a kind of détente pact, pledging that neither would allow any further attempts at mascot-napping.

Above: *Navy's Billy XV.*
USNA Archives

Above: *The Army mule mascot.*
© Ted Spiegel

game than cadets?" The superintendent jumped at the chance to explain that the law dictated the disparity in numbers between the two academies. "That," he told the president, "is one of the reasons we are getting the hell kicked out of us today."

President Kennedy, before his death in 1963, personally lobbied for passage of legislation authorizing the increase Westmoreland had long sought. Approved by Congress and signed by President Lyndon Johnson the following year, the law provided for nearly doubling the strength of the Corps by 1973. The legislation also made provision for the construction of new facilities to accommodate the expansion, including a new library, mess hall, academic building, and barracks. Though vastly increasing the size and scope of the Academy's facilities, it hardly altered the institution's historic facade as all the buildings were built in the Tudor-Gothic style so beloved by Superintendent Richard Delafield more than a century earlier.

At the same time, however, the expansion marked the beginning of an era of enormous change at West Point and in the nation at large. New stresses—an unpopular war, ideological turmoil, and racial, generational, and gender turbulence—would challenge the very fabric of the Academy and result in its transformation and renewal.

The Military Academy campus and central post area comprise only a small portion of the nearly 16,000-acre reservation.

© Ted Spiegel

In 1965 Westmoreland, by then the former superintendent, was assigned to the U.S. Military Assistance Command in South Vietnam. A different kind of conflict was being waged there, pitting the Republic of South Vietnam against the Communist insurgents known as the Vietcong in a guerrilla war without front lines. The vigorous Westmoreland seemed the right soldier to direct the escalating commitment of American air and ground forces. At West Point he had introduced a new summer program in counterinsurgency warfare known as recondo training, which combined reconnaissance and commando instruction. A New York newspaper dubbed Westmoreland "supersoldier."

New cadets (circa 1960) swear the Oath of Allegiance at Trophy Point.

But almost from the beginning, Westmoreland's military mission was ambiguous. The conduct of the war was clouded by directives from Washington that were often confusing or contradictory. As enthusiasm for the war faded back home, Westmoreland would become something of a scapegoat. "This war would stain him as it stained everything else," the journalist David Halberstam wrote. "As many of his countrymen came to doubt the war, they would come to doubt him."

At first, the cadets at West Point saw this conflict halfway around the world as an opportunity for service, promotion, and glory. Like many of their predecessors viewing combat from afar, they were eager to prove themselves worthy of the gray, and they worried that the war would end before they could graduate and get there. WE'RE IN THE BUSINESS OF WAR, proclaimed a sign someone posted, AND BUSINESS IS GOOD.

Hundreds soon had their wish. Freshly minted second lieutenants were sent to South Vietnam to command platoons engaged in the growing combat in the rice paddies, rugged mountains, and thick jungles of Vietnam. Of the sixteen thousand second lieutenants commissioned by the army in 1965 and 1966, 7 percent were new graduates of West Point. Back in Washington Hall, mess was now occasionally interrupted by the grim announcement of the death of a recent graduate. Some veterans came back to teach and tell war stories. In 1965 several alumni sent cautionary notes from the combat zone for an article in the cadet magazine. Lieutenant Bruce Heim, Class of 1963 and now with the 101st Airborne Division, wrote: "There is nothing the Army or West Point has in its training program that will prepare you to see your first dead GI, your first wounded child, your first crying widow. Military Art and Tactics never told you of the butterflies and near nausea that are continually with you as bullets fly over your head."

Members of the Class of 1966 read about the war and prepared to fight it. They were typical of the Corps during this period. The great majority came from middle-class backgrounds; almost two-thirds were sons of men who had served in the military. About two-thirds were Protestant—predominantly Episcopalian—while only 1 percent were Jewish. Three members of the class were black. Most of the 579 graduates would be sent to Vietnam. More than a hundred of them would be wounded, and thirty would lose their lives. It proved to be a higher percentage of casualties, even, than the 670-man Class of 1950, whose members fought in the Korean War.

As the war dragged on, with mounting casualties and no end in sight, disenchantment with U.S. policy—and the military itself—began to grow among the public. Members of the Class of 1966 who survived combat came home to encounter not the ticker-tape parades normally accorded heroes but stunning contempt from demonstrators who screamed, "Babykiller!" Tom Carhart, twice wounded, was strolling through Chicago's O'Hare Terminal when a group of young women darted up and spat on him. Bill Haneke, so badly mauled in Vietnam that few thought he would live, was heckled by antiwar protestors who blocked his wheelchair at Virginia Commonwealth University.

West Point itself became a refuge for cadets against the clamor of antiwar protests. Once, in 1969, the post was invaded by a hundred or so young women from Vassar College who

> " **THERE IS NOTHING THE ARMY OR WEST POINT HAS IN ITS TRAINING PROGRAM THAT WILL PREPARE YOU TO SEE YOUR FIRST DEAD GI, YOUR FIRST WOUNDED CHILD, YOUR FIRST CRYING WIDOW.** "
>
> — L I E U T E N A N T   B R U C E   H E I M

West Point Cemetery

Left: *The American Soldiers Statue (1980) honors the nation's enlisted personnel.*

© Ted Spiegel

PRESENTED TO THE CORPS OF CADETS

THE LIVES AND DESTINIES OF VALIANT AMERICANS ARE ENTRUSTED TO YOUR CARE AND LEADERSHIP

CLASS OF 1935   CLASS OF 1936

THE AMERICAN SOLDIER

Following six weeks of Beast Barracks, cadets parade past the superintendent's house in a triumphant return to campus.

© Ted Spiegel

distributed flowers to cadets, informally debated them about the war, and departed singing "America the Beautiful." Cadets took precautions when leaving the post. Some upperclassmen even kept wigs that they wore on leave to disguise their buzz cuts and blend in with their longhaired college friends. "I heard that before the war, when you walked outside the gates of the Academy you were worshipped by everybody," one bewildered cadet told a historian. "Now guys avoid wearing their uniforms when they're on leave and when you go down to march in the Armed Forces parade crowds boo you."

The national trauma induced by the Vietnam War came home to West Point most vividly one March day in 1970. At the noon meal in Washington Hall, the superintendent, Major General Samuel W. Koster, stood on the balcony known as the poop deck and faced the Corps of Cadets. Strikingly handsome, Koster was a highly respected 1942 graduate believed destined for higher promotion. But in Vietnam Koster had commanded the Americal Division, members of which committed the massacre of men, women, and children in the village of My Lai in 1968, and he was now under investigation for alleged complicity in the subsequent cover-up. He told the cadets he had requested reassignment. He ended his brief address with a gesture of defiance: "Don't let the bastards grind you down."

Many cadets leaped onto their chairs and cheered. The following day the Corps marched in homage, eyes right, past the superintendent's residence, Quarters 100, while Koster and his wife stood on the porch. A few of the cadets refused to turn but gazed straight ahead in subtle protest. Others empathized with Koster's plight but not necessarily his role in the aftermath of My Lai. "The stories in the papers made us all sound like we supported war crimes," said a Second Classman. "All we were doing with Koster was saying that we understood what it was like to get caught in the bowels of the system."

The subsequent official action against Koster, who was reduced in rank by one grade, added to the erosion of morale at the Academy. Increasing national disenchantment with the war and military service caused admissions to suffer. In the graduating classes of 1970 and 1971, less than 50 percent felt that they had made the right decision in attending the Academy—a sharp decline from 90 percent a decade previously. The disenchantment extended to the faculty. No fewer than thirty-three instructors resigned during an eighteen-month period.

Field training and summer encampments help foster a sense of teamwork and camaraderie between cadets.

© Ted Spiegel

Other political and social currents whiplashed West Point during this time of turbulence. Various trends in the nation at large threatened to undercut respect for traditional authority. Youth rebelled against their elders. College students demanded new rights and privileges and even temporarily took over some campuses. The very concept of discipline was challenged by gurus of hedonism such as Timothy Leary, the crusader for LSD who ironically had briefly been a cadet at West Point in 1940. At the same time, the institutions of the federal government—Congress, courts, the executive branch—began to intrude upon matters that Academy officials had long considered their own exclusive province.

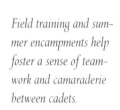

The most noticeable federal intervention occurred in racial integration. Until President Harry Truman officially integrated the armed forces by executive order in 1948 only about thirty-five African Americans had gained entry to the Academy. Though at least one black cadet was included in every incoming plebe class

A cadet hop circa 1970. Until the early 1950s, black cadets were not permitted to attend social hops.

USMA Archives

starting that year, the Academy found ways to discriminate against them until the early 1950s. They were barred from social hops and dancing classes, for example, and limited in their participation in intercollegiate sports. One black graduate later recalled that he had modified his walk and accent as a plebe in order to appear more white. "The real you was offensive to the white majority," he said. "You were accepted in accordance with how white you could become."

Civil rights legislation help prompt the Military Academy to become more open to minorities in the 1960s and 1970s.

During the late 1960s Congress pressured the service academies to fulfill the letter and spirit of the era's civil rights legislation, and at West Point in 1968, a black officer was assigned to the admissions office for the first time. The number of African American cadets, which stood at a mere thirty-six that year, also showed a dramatic increase, more than tripling in only two years. Black cadets, far from being silenced, asserted themselves. They issued a manifesto listing their grievances and successfully pressed for a course in black studies. Some even argued that the haircut regulation did not take into account the different texture and shape of black hair. "The head envisioned by the person who wrote the regulation was not a black head," a black cadet told an interviewer in 1972. "What the authorities had in mind was a blond, blue-eyed Spartan."

While civil rights concerns literally changed the complexion of the Academy—growing numbers of black faculty and staff as well as cadets joined West Point—federal courts intervened on behalf of other individual rights. By the end of his four-year tour in 1974, it was said that General William Knowlton was "the most sued Superintendent in the history of the Military Academy." Knowlton himself, on his last night on post, characterized himself as "the commander of a stockade surrounded by attacking Indians."

In one federal court suit in 1972, three cadets dismissed for "deficiencies in their military conduct" obtained the help of the American Civil Liberties Union and won reinstatement. They argued that the procedures employed to dismiss them violated the right to due process. West Point long had operated under the assumption that individuals had to surrender certain rights upon entering the Academy. Now the Academic Board met for six weeks in marathon sessions to, as someone put it, "crank due process into the system."

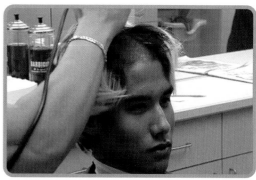

Above: *All incoming plebes receive a haircut on R-Day.*

A more stunning decision came in 1972 when the Federal courts struck down one of the Academy's oldest regulations. Since the days of Sylvanus Thayer, cadets had been required to attend weekly church services on Sunday. (The rule applied to Jewish cadets as well, even though their Sabbath occurred on Saturday; the rationale was that Christians might join a Jewish chapel held on Saturday in order to free up Sunday morning.) Mandatory chapel was "construed historically as part of man's moral formation, part of the formation of his character," said Colonel Sumner Willard, a foreign language professor. In the suit brought by two cadets and nine Naval Academy midshipmen, the justices ruled that compulsory attendance at church at the service academies violated the constitutional right to religious freedom under the First Amendment.

Below: *Cadets marching to chapel in 1966. The Federal courts ended mandatory chapel at the Academy in 1972.*
USMA Archives

Some professors at West Point likened the decision to the Vietnam War. Just as they felt the government had deprived the military of the means to carry out its mission in Vietnam, they believed West Point was now being deprived of the means to inculcate cadets with proper moral values. In their view, according to historian Joseph Ellis, who had taught at the Academy, the courts' intervention represented not only an unwarranted intrusion "but a tampering with the spiritual certification most soldiers necessarily crave."

General Andrew J. Goodpaster, who later served as superintendent, described the two-edged thrust of the Court's intervention. "The decision preserved the principles of the Constitution," he wrote, "but its effect on the Corps of Cadets was to reduce the mandatory exposure of cadets to issues of ethics and moral standards. Voluntary chapel attendance continued, but there can be little doubt (at least in the minds of many old graduates) that the change had a weakening effect in the moral-ethical sector of cadet life, with nothing of equivalent strength provided to takes its place."

The cornerstone of ethics and character is the thirteen-word honor code: "A cadet will not lie, cheat, steal, or tolerate those who do." Knowlton described the honor system as "the wellspring of all that we strive for at the Academy." In 1976 a massive cheating scandal erupted, threatening to erode the cornerstone and provoking further intrusions from authorities outside the Academy.

This was not the first time a highly publicized cheating scandal had tarnished West Point's reputation for probity. In 1951 ninety cadets resigned—including thirty-seven members of the nationally ranked varsity football team—for cheating. In 1966 forty-nine cadets were ousted for honor code violations. In 1973 a comparatively minor transgression became a cause célèbre. Cadet James Pelosi had been found guilty by the Honor Committee of "completing an answer on a quiz after the examiner had given the order to stop writing." After the superintendent reinstated Pelosi on a technicality, the Cadet Honor Committee—supported by a referendum of the entire Corps—voted to silence Pelosi, barring any conversation with the cadet outside the line of duty. When Pelosi graduated nineteen months later, the story finally surfaced in the national media, triggering charges that the honor system was inhumane and unjust. Spurred in part by the adverse publicity, the Cadet Honor Committee formally discontinued the practice of silencing cadets returned to the Academy by higher authority.

But in scope and publicity the scandal of 1976 dwarfed all previous cases. It centered on Electric Engineering 304, an unpopular course known as "juice" and despised as an exercise in "spec and dump"— memorize and forget. Because cadets often found EE304 tedious and difficult, instructors encouraged cadets to collaborate on portions of take-home assignments. On March 3 and 4, 821 Second

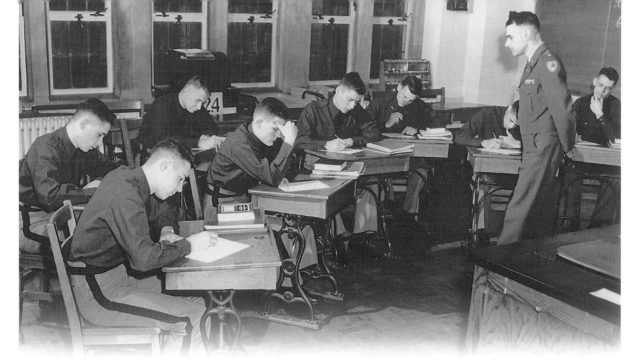

Classmen—members of the Class of 1977—received a take-home examination with four problems in designing a power supply to charge a battery or run a radio. As usual, cadets were allowed to work together on parts of the assignment but not others. The tip-off that something had gone awry was the candid note one cadet scribbled beneath his answer to a problem that had been explicitly excluded from the mutual help policy: "This computer project," he acknowledged, "does not represent all my own work. Due to the fact that I was unable to complete it on my own I received help towards its completion. I am stating this so as to avoid an unfair advantage over my classmates."

His frank confession led to an explosive inquiry that revealed widespread abuse of the Academy's honor code. Take-home assignments for EE304 had evolved from collaboration into outright plagiarism. One cadet had even painstakingly copied a doodle from the margin of another's paper, thinking it part of the answer. An initial probe brought 100 cadets before the honor committee, but further investigation identified an additional 100 suspected violators. Ultimately, a total of 152 cadets resigned or were separated from the Academy for their roles in the affair. Eventually, 92 of the dismissed cadets were granted readmission under pressure from Washington and 85 ultimately graduated.

Cadets taking a test in 1952. The Academy's first major cheating scandal occurred in 1951 and resulted in the resignation of ninety cadets.

USMA Archives

> **"A CADET WILL NOT LIE, CHEAT, STEAL, OR TOLERATE THOSE WHO DO."**
>
> — WEST POINT HONOR CODE

The scandal plunged the Academy into an agonizing period of analysis and reevaluation—and scorching outside scrutiny. Everyone, it seemed, could cite a possible cause: West Point's highly pressurized academic environment, cynicism toward authority nationwide; some even argued that the vast expansion of the Corps won by Westmoreland had made West Point impersonal and unwieldy. To examine the affair in depth,

Secretary of the Army Martin Hoffmann appointed an outside commission headed by the former astronaut Frank Borman, Class of 1950 and president of Eastern Airlines. The Borman Commission found in the Corps a disaffection with the honor code that bordered on contempt—"cool on honor" was the cadet expression. "The Academy must now acknowledge the causes of the breakdown and devote its full energies to rebuilding an improved and strengthened institution."

The year of the scandal, 1976, also marked the celebration of the nation's bicentennial. On July 4, thousands of cadets and civilians from throughout the Hudson Valley gathered to watch the spectacular fireworks display scheduled at West Point. As dark descended, a technician ignited the first skyrocket. It rose a few feet, sputtered, and tumbled to the ground. The arsenal of fireworks had somehow gotten wet, and one by one, the spiderwebs, golden dragons, and other pyrotechnic wonders fizzled. It seemed an appropriate metaphor for the Academy's depressed mood. West Point, someone remarked, could not even keep its powder dry for a simple birthday party.

Three days after the great fireworks fizzle, a new challenge confronted the Academy. With the impact of Vietnam still fresh, with authorities still reeling from the worst cheating scandal ever, West Point welcomed a new class of plebes. This group was not merely raw and undisciplined like all new recruits; it included the first 119 women ever admitted to the Academy.

As recently as two years previously, the very notion of women at West Point seemed unthinkable. Most West Pointers viewed the notion with even more dismay than an earlier generation had greeted the arrival of the school's first black cadet. Each of the service secretaries and uniformed chiefs had issued statements adamantly opposing it. They asserted women could not meet the rigorous physical and emotional standards of the service academies. They also suggested it would make no sense to train female combat leaders when the public would never accept women in combat. Westmoreland, the former super-intendent, Vietnam commander, and army chief of staff, called the whole idea "silly." He added, "Maybe you could find one woman in ten thousand who could lead in combat, but she would be a freak and we're not running the Military Academy for freaks."

But such all-male citadels as Yale and Princeton had opened their doors to both sexes, and political pressure on behalf of gender equality was mounting throughout American society. With the end of the draft and the advent of the volunteer army in the last stages of the Vietnam experience, opportunities for women were broadened in an attempt to maintain the quality of the services. As women's opportunities expanded throughout the military, it seemed appropriate to admit them to the service academies as well.

When President Gerald Ford signed the legislation in October 1975, West Point's superintendent, Major General Sidney B. Berry, briefly thought about resigning in protest rather than preside over the admission of women. A member of the Class of 1948 and the recipient of four Silver Stars and two Purple Hearts for service in Korea and Vietnam, Berry possessed an impeccable record. The cheating scandal would unavoidably tarnish that record, but few could fault his role in gender integration. He knew his duty, he told a journalist; he ultimately decided to put his opposition to women at West Point "behind me and do what the good soldier does."

For the next nine months, he and his administration threw themselves into "the advance preparation normally given to an important, well-planned military maneuver,"— as the Office of Public Affairs put it. Seeking applicants, the admissions office wrote thousands of high school counselors across the country. In December three hundred cadets were sent home two days early on Christmas leave to corral qualified women applicants in their hometowns. Among the 6,761 nominees for entry in 1976, nearly 10 percent were women; 148 were offered admission, and 119 became members of the Class of 1980.

Plebes from the Class of 1980 (the first to include women) prepare for "Recognition" by the upper classes. At this ceremony upperclassmen address the plebes by their first names for the first time.
© Ted Spiegel

The Academy, meanwhile, studied other institutions, such as the Merchant Marine Academy, that had recently gone coeducational. Officials established procedures for issues ranging from the folding of brassieres to dealing with menstrual cycles in the field. Berry reserved for himself the approval of any standards that differed from the norm for male cadets. He decided that instead of the normal mandatory physical education courses in boxing and wrestling, which might cause breast injuries, women would take a two-semester course in martial arts. Their hair could be long enough to reach the bottom of the collar. They could wear makeup and perfume, Berry ruled, in "tasteful moderation."

Fashion designers from Hart Schaffner & Marx arrived to consult on uniforms to better accommodate female anatomy. The tails on the traditional full-dress tunic, it turned out, ballooned unbecomingly around a woman's hips. After watching models parade by in varying styles, Berry made what he called "a major command decision." Tails on women's coats would be cut off, creating a style like an Eisenhower jacket. One of the new cadets, Carol Barkalow, later put it bluntly in her book *In the Men's House:* "Our Full Dress coats were cut off at the waist for fear that our derrieres would appear too prominent during parades. Of course, the difference between the uniforms only accentuated what the Academy wanted us to conceal. It would be three years before the authorities relented and gave us coats with tails."

A female cadet leads exercises on the Plain. Despite initial resistance by the all-male Corps of Cadets, women now constitute about 15 percent of the student body.

Hoping to psychologically prepare male cadets, Berry and two other generals at the Academy convened a series of question-and-answer sessions informally known as Stump

© Ted Spiegel

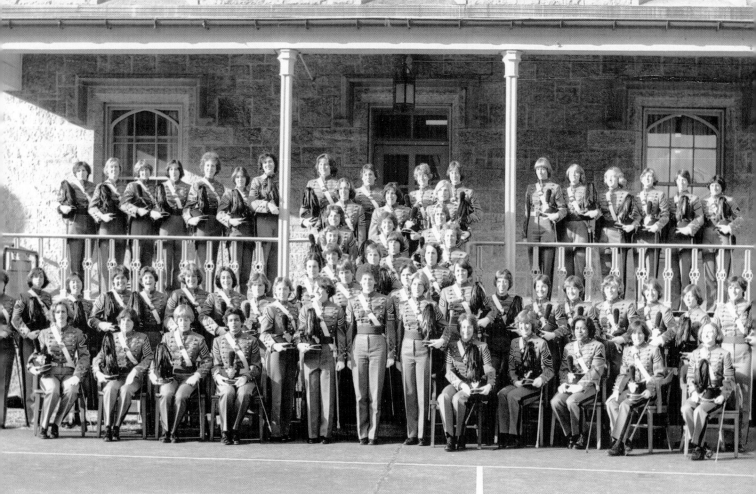

The first female cadets (Class of 1980) to graduate from the Academy.

the Stars. The prevailing mood among the young men was doubtless predictable given the opinions already publicly expressed by the Army's highest-ranking officers. Cadet hostility surfaced in the meetings and in surveys conducted by the Academy. It far exceeded the mere chauvinism shown by the 40 percent in a survey who agreed that "A woman's activities are best confined in the home." One cadet said flatly, "I think it is a disgrace for women to be here." Another wrote, "I feel it is my duty to the alumni and the entire Army to run out as many females as possible."

The hostility spilled over into actual harassment and abuse after the women took up residence at West Point. The harsh treatment extended beyond the usual hazing of plebes. Male cadets vandalized their rooms. Upperclassmen in one company organized a contest to reduce every woman in the company to tears at least once. Some cadets scrawled crude sexual slurs on barracks walls. They made fun of women who gained excessive weight on the 4,000-calorie-a-day mess-hall fare. They addressed female cadets as whores and bitches and made elaborate attempts to identify any possible lesbians. "We seemed to be continually stuck in a tiresome stereotype," wrote Carol Barkalow of that first year. "If we were not socializing heavily with male cadets, then it meant we must be lesbians. If we were socializing heavily with male cadets, then it meant we must be whores."

BECOMING
A CADET

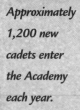

Approximately 1,200 new cadets enter the Academy each year.

© Robert Stewart

The United States Military Academy was established in 1802 with a total of ten cadets, all appointed by President Thomas Jefferson. Today the Corps of Cadets numbers approximately four thousand men and women who come from every state and territory of the country and are admitted through a unique system of nomination, qualification, evaluation, and selection.

"The long gray line, a phrase that has real meaning to a cadet, means that linkage from cadets of two hundred years ago with the cadets of two hundred years from now," says General David Palmer, former superintendent and historian of West Point's early years.

Applicants today must first be nominated by an authorized source in order to be considered for appointment. The president, vice president, secretary of the army, and all members of Congress may nominate individuals. Other nomination channels exist for enlisted military personnel and children of deceased or disabled military personnel. Applicants cannot be married, pregnant, or have a legal obligation to support a child or children. Cadets must be between the ages of seventeen and twenty-three upon entry to the Academy.

Prospective cadets are evaluated in three areas: academic performance (high school record and SAT or ACT scores), demonstrated leadership potential, and physical aptitude. The physical aptitude examination consists of four events: pull-ups for men or flexed-arm hang for women; a basketball throw from a kneeling position; the standing long jump; and a three-hundred-yard shuttle run. Applicants must pass the physical exam to be admitted to West Point.

Once they become cadets, women are required to meet the same standards as their male counterparts in academics, leadership, and military development. The only exception is that women are required to take self-defense courses, rather than boxing and wrestling, in their first and second years.

West Point graduates earn a bachelor of science degree and are commissioned as second lieutenants in the U.S. Army. Graduates must serve at least five years of active duty and three years in a Reserve Component, a total of eight years. The active duty obligation is the nation's return on a West Point graduate's fully funded, four-year college education—currently valued in excess of $250,000.

General Goodpaster later observed that the "undercurrent of resentment and opposition among male cadets and officers at West Point" extended to many graduates. "This problem remained a source of concern and added to the disruptive, divisive, and unresponsive tendencies among cadets and the whole West Point community."

The Academy had to cope with attraction as well as repulsion. New regulations allowed dating between upperclassmen and between plebes but not between upperclassmen and plebes. The fact that both men and women were housed on the same corridors in the barracks demanded the vigilance of tactical officers. At least one officer put masking tape on the floor to mark just how far doors should be left open in cadet rooms when both sexes were present. Public Displays of Affection—PDAs—such as holding hands were prohibited. Those caught engaging in actual sexual intimacy were marched before what cadets called the

Pershing Barracks is one of several barracks on campus that house the Corps of Cadets. Men and women live in separate rooms but on integrated floors.

" [THE] UNDERCURRENT OF RESENTMENT AND OPPOSITION AMONG MALE CADETS AND OFFICERS AT WEST POINT . . . REMAINED A SOURCE OF CONCERN AND ADDED TO THE DISRUPTIVE, DIVISIVE, AND UNRESPONSIVE TENDENCIES AMONG CADETS AND THE WHOLE WEST POINT COMMUNITY."

— GENERAL ANDREW J. GOODPASTER

"fornication board" and harshly punished for "engaging in acts of affection prejudicial to the discipline and good order of the U.S. Corps of Cadets."

The women managed to gain a measure of grudging respect with their performance in the athletic arena. By 1978 West Point fielded nine women's intercollegiate teams and turned in winning seasons with all of them. That was the third year for the Academy's first group of women, and they happily embraced the nickname traditionally given to Second Classmen—cows. A female cadet of a later generation observed, "This must be the only institution where it's okay for female students to be called cows."

Fierce resentment against women cadets did not begin to ease until the graduation of the Academy's last all-male class in 1979. Much to the surprise of many men, more than half of the original group of women—sixty-two of them—survived to graduate in 1980, and the granite towers did not crumble. Indeed, the only member of the class, male or female, to receive the much-prized Rhodes Scholarship was Andrea Hollen.

In the remaining years of the Academy's second century of existence, the Corps of Cadets increasingly reflected the rich mosaic of the American people. Milestones in this diversity came with the selection of the first captain of the Corps—the highest cadet rank and the honor previously earned by such storied graduates as John Pershing and Douglas MacArthur. In the Class of 1976, the first captain was a Hispanic American, Richard Morales Jr.; in 1980, an African American, Vincent Brooks; in 1987, an Asian American, John Tien Jr.; in 1990, a woman, Kristin Baker. By the end of West Point's second century, 15 percent of the Corps was female and 9 percent black.

Cadet Kristin Baker, Class of 1990, was the first woman to become first captain of the Corps. She is shown here assisting the Oldest Graduate Present in placing a wreath at the Thayer Statue.

In addition to all the other challenges during these years, West Point had to confront the need for change academically. Ever since Thayer, superintendents have attempted to maintain the delicate balance between the Academy's two distinct aspects: It is both an undergraduate college and a professional school for training army officers—in the familiar phrase, "both Athens and Sparta." During the decades after World War II, shortcomings in its Athenian academic role once again came under attack from critics within and without. One college professor who had studied the Academy and found it wanting gave cadets a backhanded compliment: "West Point is a second-class college for first-class students."

Academic reform gathered momentum during the late 1950s under Superintendent Garrison Davidson. Known to his colleagues as Gar, Davidson, Class of 1927, had successfully coached the football team for five years in the 1930s. During World War II he had so impressed General Patton with his battlefield brilliance that Patton, in promoting Davidson, had personally

Taylor Hall serves as the headquarters for the USMA administration.
© Bob Krist

pinned a pair of his own stars on him. Davidson believed that West Point had to go beyond the old Thayer curriculum dominated by mathematics and engineering and become, once again, a first-rate academic institution. "The time has come," he wrote in 1957, "for a more searching and fundamental review of what our goals should be and how to attain them."

Keenly aware of the sensitive nature of any change at the Academy, he proceeded cautiously. He disarmed potential opponents by seeking their advice. He appointed special study groups and committees. Never had so many members of the major constituencies— staff, faculty, alumni, and even cadets—been engaged in such an intensive review of Academy programs. Davidson could decree certain changes. For example, he established a program of sabbatical leaves to encourage intellectual development and urged faculty to publish in professional journals. Permanent professors would now be expected to obtain their doctorates.

In order to effect change in the curriculum, however, Davidson had to deal with the official body that had frustrated so many of his predecessors: the Academic Board.

Davidson, among other things, wanted to introduce elective courses into the curriculum and to increase the emphasis on social sciences and humanities. A sample of the Academic Board's traditional resistance to electives had been given a few years before by a professor who argued that each cadet "has exercised a complete freedom of choice in his decision to come to West Point at all—he chose the prescribed curriculum." In early 1960, after months of agonized discussion over Davidson's proposals to liberalize the curriculum, the board met for five successive days to consider the issue of electives. "Intense to say the least—but friendly," Davidson said of the discussions. "Blood was drawn but the wounded lived."

> **" THE TIME HAS COME FOR A MORE SEARCHING AND FUNDAMENTAL REVIEW OF WHAT OUR GOALS SHOULD BE AND HOW TO ATTAIN THEM. "**
>
> – SUPERINTENDENT GAR DAVIDSON

Davidson managed only a partial victory—approval for cadets to take one elective during each of their two semesters in the final year. But his efforts initiated an era of enduring efforts at academic reform. The number of electives available to cadets was repeatedly increased, allowing them to take advanced courses in mathematics, English, and foreign languages.

The cheating scandal of 1976 led to new reforms. In the wake of the Borman Commission investigation, the army chief of staff appointed the West Point Study Group to evaluate every aspect of the Academy. A key result was the recommendation to strengthen the authority of the superintendent at the expense of the Academic Board. General Andrew Goodpaster, Class of 1939 and Eisenhower's former staff secretary in the White House, who was brought back from retirement to serve as superintendent, implemented this and other major changes, and reform moved ahead more rapidly. In the new forty-course curriculum, ten courses were electives. Then, in 1982, sixteen optional majors were finally introduced to allow cadets to pursue special interests rather than have all cadets follow the traditional math-science-engineering–oriented curriculum.

Lieutenant General Garrison "Gar" Davidson (Class of 1927) took over the superintendency in 1956.

Other significant reforms accompanied the academic changes. An emphasis on what Goodpaster called "positive leadership" formally replaced hazing, which was newly defined as "abusive and inappropriate leadership." Over time new regulations have forbidden exaggerated forms such as bracing, "pinging", and "squaring corners" (rushing from place to place and making ninety-degree turns anytime a cadet changes course while walking). "Each year it becomes more professional," Cadet Michelle Timajo, Class of 2001,

said of the old Beast Barracks, "and they lean more toward a low tone, that is, talking instead of screaming right at you. There is no physical hazing, and even verbal hazing now takes the form more of making corrections when someone messes up rather than simply yelling at plebes."

The honor system, which had been called into question by the cheating scandal of 1976, was strengthened and remains a bedrock of education in character. Official recognition that cadets did not enter the Academy possessed of a fully developed moral compass led to a four-year program of instruction in ethics and honor. These courses, for example, show how the concepts of Duty, Honor, and Country have evolved to permit the disobeying of an order that is clearly a violation of the duties of a professional soldier and international law. A blue-ribbon outside commission appointed in 1988 to review the Academy's honor code concluded that it was "an example for all public service." The code, declared the panel, "represents a standard of ethical behavior that functions effectively for cadets, to which American professionals can aspire, and which all citizens should appreciate as a national asset."

The successful efforts at renewal gave the lie to charges that West Point had plenty of tradition to show but little progress. In 1999, in a new edition of *The Long Gray Line*, his

The Corps of Cadets gathers on the Plain for a Taps Vigil in remembrance of the victims of the September 11, 2001 terrorist attacks.

Tom Bushey/
The Times Herald-Record

General Norman Schwarzkopf returned to the Academy for a visit after successfully leading troops in Operation Desert Storm.

account of the Class of 1966 and the travails experienced by West Point, Rick Atkinson remarked on the impressive advances made by the Academy in subsequent years. "No longer could West Point fairly be said to represent two centuries of tradition unhampered by progress," he wrote. "Change—gradual but relentless as the glaciers that carved the Hudson Valley—continued through the 1990s."

Not the least of that progress resulted from the resurgence of American pride in the military profession after its sad decline during the Vietnam War. In 1991 U.S. forces played a prominent role in Operation Desert Storm, the campaign by an allied coalition that swiftly crushed the Iraqi army, reversing its invasion of neighboring Kuwait. West Point could cite the gallantry and battlefield

" [WEST POINT] GAVE ME FAR MORE THAN A MILITARY CAREER—IT GAVE ME A CALLING."

— G E N E R A L   H .   N O R M A N   S C H W A R Z K O P F

leadership of its male and female graduates, including the commander of Desert Storm, Lieutenant General H. Norman Schwarzkopf. "It was exactly the war that the U.S. military had been training to fight for 40 years and we were good." said Schwarzkopf. And, he added, "it did serve on the part of a lot of us to expunge the ghosts of Vietnam."

Schwarzkopf felt that he has been practically born into the Academy. "West Point has been part of my consciousness as long as I can remember," he said. His father graduated in the Class of 1917, later organized the New Jersey State Police, and was called back during World War II, retiring as a major general. The younger Schwarzkopf graduated in the top 10 percent of the Class of 1956 and flirted with the air force before settling for the infantry. He twice was assigned as an instructor at West Point and served two tours with distinction in Vietnam, which only strengthened his sense of duty. "When I began as a plebe," he recalled in his best-selling memoir *It Doesn't Take a Hero*, "'Duty, Honor, Country' was just a motto I'd heard from Pop. By the time I left, those values had become my fixed stars. Some officers spend all their time currying favor and worrying about the next promotion—a miserable way to live. But West Point saved me from that by instilling the ideal of service above self. It gave me far more than a military career—it gave me a calling."

The precise nature of that calling in West Point's third century cannot be predicted. Along with the mission of the army itself, the role of the long gray line in the post–Cold War world changes and expands, embracing preparation for such tasks as peacekeeping and humanitarian assistance as well as fighting wars and brushfires. As it has since its founding by Thomas Jefferson in 1802, West Point intends to go on meeting the challenge of producing leaders of character committed to Duty, Honor, Country.

As the U.S. Military Academy celebrates its bicentennial in 2002, it continues to press forward with its mission "To educate, train, and inspire the Corps of Cadets so that each graduate is a commissioned leader of character committed to the values of Duty, Honor, Country; professional growth throughout a career as an officer in the United States Army; and a lifetime of selfless service to the nation."

© Ted Spiegel

CHRONOLOGICAL HISTORY
of the United States Military Academy

1802

The United States Military Academy is established by an act of Congress of March 16. The law directs that the Corps of Engineers "shall constitute a military academy." The West Point site is selected because of economy, convenience, and its historically rich association with the American Revolution.

Jonathan Williams, grandnephew of Benjamin Franklin, becomes the Academy's first superintendent. The Academy is limited to ten cadets.

1803

A teacher of French and a teacher of drawing are authorized for the Military Academy.

1812

An act of Congress sets the size of the Corps of Cadets at 250, and establishes basic entrance requirements and qualifications for cadets. The law also provides for the employment of a number of enlisted musicians who form the nucleus of the USMA Band, now the oldest army band in the nation.

The USMA Band was established in 1812.

At the outbreak of the War of 1812, there are only eighty-eight graduates of the Military Academy, but sixty-five are in military service. For their contributions in the war,

Dr. Stephen Grove, USMA Historian

Henry Adams offers the tribute: "During the critical campaign of 1814, the West Point engineers doubled the capacity of the little American army for resistance, and introduced a new and scientific character into American life."

1815

Alden Partridge, an 1806 graduate, becomes acting superintendent. His short tenure is controversial and after his departure he becomes a critic of the Military Academy. Because of later work and service as head of Norwich Academy, he is often called the Father of ROTC.

1816

Gray is adopted as the color of the cadet uniform. Gray is chosen, rather than the blue normally used for the regular army troops, because it is less expensive. Later it will erroneously be said to have been chosen in honor of the victory of Winfield Scott's gray-clad regulars at the Battle of Chippewa in the War of 1812.

1817

Sylvanus Thayer, an 1808 graduate, takes command of the Military Academy. Thayer establishes the principle of strict adherence to the rule of discipline and advancement according to merit as basic tenets of a military education.

The West Point Cemetery is officially established.

West Point circa 1780

National Archives

1819—1942

Clinton Field, immediately west of Fort Clinton, serves as the site of cadet summer camps from 1819 until 1942. Fort Clinton had originally been called Fort Arnold; after Arnold's treason, however, the name was changed to honor the Revolutionary War patriot General James Clinton.

1820

The superintendent's quarters are completed. Colonel Thayer is the first superintendent to live there.

1828

The Kosciuszko Monument is given by the Corps of Cadets in honor of Colonel Thaddeus Kosciuszko, the Polish patriot who supervised the construction of fortifications at West Point during the Revolutionary War.

1829

The West Point Hotel is built on the northern edge of the Plain overlooking the Hudson River.

1833

Colonel Thayer is relieved from duty as superintendent at his own request. His successful administration earned him the title Father of the Military Academy.

1835

West Point's Class of 1835 originates the class ring custom now followed at thousands of universities across the country.

Cadets return from Ring Ceremony at Trophy Point.

© Ted Spiegel

1836

The construction of the Old Cadet Chapel is completed in the main cadet area. In 1911, as the Academy later expands and a new chapel is constructed, this chapel will be relocated to its present site at the entrance to the cemetery, where it will be used as a mortuary chapel.

1838

An act of Congress makes the total term of military service eight years, thus ensuring the government four years of service in return for four years of education.

"Benny Havens, O!" first appears in the *Army and Navy Chronicle*. The poem, sung to the tune of "Wearing of the Green," celebrates the escapades at the Benny Havens tavern—which will be known to succeeding generations of cadets long after it closes its doors just after the Civil War.

1843

Congress passes a law specifying that the Corps of Cadets will consist of one cadet from each congressional district, establishing the Academy's national character.

1845—1851

New barracks are built and constitute a section of what will later be known as Central Barracks.

1846—1848

Military successes in the Mexican War establish national confidence in West Point training.

1854

The West Point Museum is founded. Now located at Olmsted Hall at Pershing Center, the collection memorializes all of the nation's, and many of the world's, military conflicts.

The Military Academy's course of study is lengthened from four to five years. The class that enters in June 1854 is divided into two parts according to age; the younger portion is the first group to follow the five-year curriculum.

1857

An act of Congress authorizes the appointment of a professor of Spanish.

1858

The Academy's course of study returns to four years. In 1859 it will go back to five years, but in 1861 it will return to four years.

1861–1865

The performance of Military Academy graduates in the Civil War establishes the institution in the national consciousness. The Academy provides more than four hundred generals to lead both the North and South.

1866

An act of Congress provides that the superintendent of the Military Academy may "hereafter be selected, and the officers on duty at the Institution detailed from any arm of the service." The law recognizes the fact that the Academy is no longer merely a school of engineering and removes control of the institution from the Corps of Engineers.

1868

A statue is dedicated in memory of Major General John Sedgwick, commander of the Sixth Army Corps, who fell in the Battle of Spotsylvania.

1869

A meeting is held to organize the Association of Graduates of the U.S. Military Academy, the alumni association. This event brings together military leaders of both the North and South.

Fan autographed by members of the Classes of 1867, 1868, and 1869

West Point Museum Collections, USMA

1877

Henry O. Flipper becomes the first African American to graduate from the U.S. Military Academy.

1880

A YMCA branch is formed at West Point. This will become the largest and most influential cadet extracurricular organization, until it is dissolved in 1933.

1883

The Thayer Monument, dedicated to Colonel Sylvanus Thayer, the Father of the Military Academy, is erected.

1884

The *Howitzer* is first published. The volume includes the program of jokes, poems, and stories of the Hundredth Night celebration. In 1896 the *Howitzer* will change its format and combine with the cadet album to become the cadet yearbook. It will receive official Academy sanction in 1904, one of the first in the nation.

Hundredth Night celebrations have been a tradition at West Point since the mid-1800s.

1885

Herman J. Koehler, later called the Father of Army Physical Education, is appointed Master of the Sword and stimulates greater attention to athletics and physical fitness at West Point.

1887

Following the death of Ulysses S. Grant, Class of 1843, two years before, the cadet dining hall is renamed Grant Hall.

1890

The first Army-Navy football game is played at West Point. The Military Academy enters the field of intercollegiate athletic competition.

1895

The West Academic Building is completed. Pershing Barracks is now located on the site.

1897

Battle Monument is erected. Located at Trophy Point, it is dedicated to the memory of the 2,230 soldiers and officers of the regular army killed in action in the Civil War. An architectural engineering firm headed by Stanford White designed the monument.

1898

The West Point motto "Duty, Honor, Country" is selected, and a coat of arms and Academy seal are adopted.

Cullum Memorial Hall is completed. Named for
Major General George W. Cullum, Class of 1833,
superintendent 1864–1866, the facility will
serve as an alumni hall for nearly a century.

1899

The colors black,
gray, and gold are
adopted as the colors
of the U.S. Military
Academy for use in all
athletic games.

Elihu Root, secretary
of war, praises the
Academy's contribution
in the Spanish-American
War: "I believe that the great service which it has
rendered the country was never more conspicuous than it
has been during the past two years."

1900

The size of the Corps of Cadets is 481.

The Chapel of Most Holy Trinity is completed.

1901

An act of Congress forbids hazing.

1902

President Theodore Roosevelt is the guest of honor at the
Military Academy centennial.

Herbert S. Shipman, USMA chaplain, writes "The Corps,"
the Academy's inspiring anthem, for the centennial.

1903

The West Point Army Mess (later designated the Officers'
Club and even later the Community Club) is completed.

1905

Boxing and wrestling are added to the physical education
curriculum.

1906

For the first time, all four classes
participate in physical
education and training.

*General Jonathan M. Wainwright
(Class of 1906) memorabilia from
WWII*

West Point Museum Collections, USMA

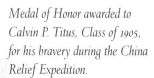

*Medal of Honor awarded to
Calvin P. Titus, Class of 1905,
for his bravery during the China
Relief Expedition.*

West Point Museum Collections, USMA

1907

Bugle Notes, the cadet handbook, is first
published as a YMCA project.

1908

North Barracks is completed in the Tudor-Gothic style of
architecture. The architectural engineering firm of Cram,
Goodhue, and Ferguson—which won a national
competition for the Academy's major building program—
designed the structure. Over the next several years, the firm
will use the Gothic style in the design of the Administration
Building, the Cadet Chapel, the East Gymnasium, the
Riding Hall, and the East Academic Building.

1909

Constitution Island is donated to the government (Military
Academy) by Miss Anna Warner through Mrs. Russell Sage.

The Administration Building is completed. It contains the
offices of the superintendent, the dean of the Academic
Board, and the general staff.

1910

The Cadet Chapel
is completed.
Located west of,
and 300 feet
above, the cadet
barracks, it
dominates the
Plain. The chapel
organ, with more
than twenty-two
thousand pipes, is reputed to be the largest church organ in
the world.

The East Gymnasium is completed.

1911

The Riding Hall is completed. In
1959 it will be converted into Thayer
Hall, an academic building.

"Alma Mater" is first sung as hymn.

1913

The East Academic Building is completed; it will later be renamed Bartlett Hall.

1916

The Washington Monument is erected.

The authorized strength of the Corps of Cadets increases to 1,332.

1917—1918

Academy graduates serve as thirty-four of the thirty-eight corps and division commanders in the First World War. John J. Pershing of the Class of 1886 leads the American Expeditionary Force (AEF).

The Academy's course of instruction compresses to produce officers more rapidly for the war.

1919

The French Cadet Monument, a gift of L'Ecole Polytechnique, is erected.

1919—1922

General MacArthur serves as Academy superintendent. Under his direction, the course of instruction returns to a four-year program. He also establishes an extensive intramural athletic program for all classes. He composes the lines: "Upon the fields of friendly strife are sown the seeds that, upon other fields, on other days, will bear the fruits of victory."

Major Robert M. Danford, commandant of cadets, introduces a course on leadership. As an aid in the appointment of cadet officers and noncommissioned officers in an enlarged Corps, he devises and uses a system of efficiency ratings of cadets by cadets.

1924

Michie Stadium is completed. The football stadium is named for First Lieutenant Dennis Mahan Michie, Class of 1892, captain of the first West Point football team, who was killed in action at San Juan Hill, Cuba, in 1898.

1926

The government-owned Hotel Thayer is completed. An addition in 1948 will provide accommodations for five hundred guests. It is the only place where any visitor can stay on the West Point grounds.

1929

Washington Hall is completed. Arnold Brunner and Associates construct it in the traditional Tudor-Gothic style. It includes the Cadet Dining Hall and has a seating capacity of twenty-five hundred. With the subsequent expansion of the Corps in the late 1960s and early 1970s, Washington Hall will be expanded to a seating capacity of forty-four hundred. The offices of the commandant and his staff and the Departments of Military Instruction and Foreign Languages also are located in this structure.

1931

A new Grant Hall is completed on the site of a previous Grant Hall (Cadet Mess Hall). It is a cadet reception hall and contains the office of the cadet hostess.

1933

An act of Congress authorizes awarding the bachelor of science degree to Academy graduates.

1936—1942

The Academy acquires additional territory to the west and south for tactical military training.

1939

Doubleday Field is named in honor of Major General Abner Doubleday, Class of 1842, who is said to have laid out the first modern baseball diamond at Cooperstown, New York, in 1839.

1941

German language study is introduced.

1941–1945

Academy graduates including Generals Dwight Eisenhower (Class of 1915), Douglas MacArthur (1903), Omar Bradley (1915), and George Patton (1909) lead the Allies to victory in World War II.

1942

Air corps branch instruction is instituted at the Military Academy. This action requires the division of classes into two groups: air and ground cadets.

1943

A three-year course of instruction is adapted due to the requirements for additional officers in World War II.

1944–1946

West Point enjoys the glory years of Army football under Coach Earl H. "Red" Blaik and Heisman Trophy winners "Doc" Blanchard and Glenn Davis.

West Point football today

1945

The Tactical Training and Firing Center, used for the summer training of cadets, is named Camp Buckner in honor of Lieutenant General Simon Bolivar Buckner Jr., Class of 1908, killed at Okinawa.

Russian language study is introduced.

1946

Under Major General Maxwell D. Taylor, superintendent, the Academy curriculum is revised and modernized. Formal leadership instruction is provided by what will later become the Department of Behavioral Sciences and Leadership.

1947

New instructors are designated before their actual assignment to West Point so they may attend civilian universities for graduate work and to receive advanced degrees.

1950

The George S. Patton Jr. Monument is dedicated. This monument was "erected by his friends, officers and men of the units he commanded."

The George S. Patton Jr. Monument

1955

The patriotic movie *Long Gray Line,* featuring the career of Sergeant Marty Maher, is released.

1956

The weekly CBS television series *West Point* begins in October. Viewed by an estimated twenty-five million weekly, the program contributes to an increased flow of visitors to West Point and more candidates competing for vacancies at the U.S. Military Academy.

1957

Project Equality establishes an even distribution of scholastic ability, physical ability, leadership potential, and height across all cadet companies. The policy is initiated with the entering Class of 1961.

1959

The positions of chairman of the athletic board, director of athletics, and head football coach, previously concentrated in one individual, are divided into separate positions following the resignation of Coach Earl H. "Red" Blaik after eighteen years of service at West Point.

The Riding Hall is converted into Thayer Hall, an academic building.

Mahan Hall
© Ted Spiegel

1961

USMA is designated an official national historical landmark.

1962

On May 12, General of the Army Douglas MacArthur accepts the Thayer Award and delivers his famous "Duty, Honor, Country" speech.

1964

President Johnson signs a law that provides for an Academy expansion almost doubling the size of the Corps of Cadets to forty-four hundred by 1973.

A new library is completed with a storage capacity of half a million volumes.

Plebes are allowed to go home for Christmas for the first time.

1965

Colonel Edward H. White II, Class of 1952, becomes the first American to walk in space.

"Plebe Parent Weekend," an orientation program for parents of plebes, is begun during spring leave.

Groundbreaking ceremonies for the new Washington Hall Barracks complex are held. The complex is needed to accommodate the expansion of the Corps.

The First Division of old Central Barracks, previously occupied by cadet first captains such as Pershing and MacArthur, will be preserved.

1966

The study of Mandarin Chinese begins.

1969

MacArthur Memorial and Barracks are dedicated.

1973

The Supreme Court ends mandatory chapel at the Military Academy.

Cavalry Plain is renamed Buffalo Soldier Field.

Mahan Hall, named in honor of the famous military engineer Dennis Hart Mahan, Class of 1824, is completed. It is the site of most Academy engineering departments.

The Cadet Honor Committee acts to eliminate silencing under the honor system.

1974

The Cadet Activities Center (Eisenhower Hall) opens.

1976

Women cadets are first admitted to the Military Academy.

The Borman Commission Report reviews the state of honor at West Point.

Arabic language instruction is added to the curriculum.

1977

The West Point Study Group Report is released. The report reviews all aspects of the Academy program and policies.

General Andrew J. Goodpaster, Class of 1939, comes out of retirement to serve as Academy superintendent. During his superintendency, the Academy embarks upon a comprehensive review of academic policies and practices and adopts most of the recommendations of the West Point Study Group Report.

1980

The first women graduate from the Military Academy.

Andrea Hollen, Class of 1980, was the Academy's first female graduate.

West Point Museum Collections, USMA

1981

A formal Honor Education Program is created.

1982

The Academy's Academic Board adopts a program of optional majors for cadets beginning with the Class of 1985.

1983

The Eisenhower Monument is dedicated.

1984

The Academy formally acquires the old Ladycliff College (South Post) property.

The Jewish Chapel conducts its first services

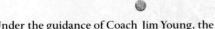

Under the guidance of Coach Jim Young, the football team wins the Commander in Chief Trophy and ranks among the top twenty American football teams for the first time in two decades.

1985

The first engineering programs receive accreditation by the Accreditation Board of Engineering and Technology (ABET).

The Multi-Purpose Sports Complex opens for basketball and hockey. The facility will later be named the Holleder Center for Don Holleder (Class of 1956), an accomplished scholar-athlete killed in action in Vietnam.

1986

Kevin Houston, the Military Academy's all-time leading scorer, becomes the first college basketball player in the nation to have both the highest scoring average and the highest free-throw percentage.

1988

USMA begins a graduate program in leader development for future tactical officers.

1989

The Posvar Commission Report finds the honor code an "exemplar for all public services" and issues a "call for its extension throughout the Army, the government and American society as a whole."

The new Museum and Visitors Center opens to the public at South Post (later Pershing Center).

1989

Cadet Kristin Baker becomes the first woman to serve as the brigade commander (first captain).

1990

The traditional Fourth Class system is superseded by the Cadet Leader Development System (CLDS).

1991

General H. Norman Schwarzkopf, Class of 1956, leads Operation Desert Storm. Three young graduates of the Military Academy are lost in that conflict.

The thousandth black and the thousandth woman graduate from the Military Academy.

1993

Passage of FY93 Defense Appropriation Bill calls for the reduction in the size of the Corps of Cadets to four thousand by 1996 and an increase in civilian faculty to 25 percent by the year 2002.

2002

The nation observes the Academy's bicentennial.

© Ted Spiegel

SOURCE ACKNOWLEDGMENTS

In writing *West Point: The First 200 Years*, three excellent books were referred to extensively as sources of quoted material in all seven chapters. They are Stephen E. Ambrose's *Duty, Honor, Country*, Theodore J. Crackel's *The Illustrated History of West Point*, and George S. Pappas's *To the Point*. The author and the publisher gratefully acknowledge the fine research work of these historians. In addition, the following publications were used extensively as sources for quotes in specific chapters:

Chapter 3: "Cadet Life before the Mexican War," edited by Sidney Forman.

Chapter 4: *Personal Memoirs of U. S. Grant*, by Ulysses S. Grant; *Lee and Grant*, by Gene Smith; *The Class of 1846*, by John C. Waugh.

Chapter 5: *West Point*, by Thomas J. Fleming; *Bullies and Cowards*, by Philip W. Leon.

Chapter 6: *West Point*, by Thomas J. Fleming; *The Years of MacArthur*, by D. Clayton James.

Chapter 7: *The Long Gray Line*, by Rick Atkinson; *School for Soldiers*, by Joseph Ellis and Robert Moore.

The extensive interviews conducted for the West Point television special also provided valuable source material in compiling this book.

BIBLIOGRAPHY

Ambrose, Stephen E. *Duty, Honor, Country: A History of West Point*. Baltimore: Johns Hopkins University Press, 1966, 1999.

————. *Eisenhower*, vol. 1. New York: Simon & Schuster, 1984.

Arnold, Henry H. *Global Mission* (Military Classics Series). New York: Harper, 1949.

Atkinson, Rick. *The Long Gray Line: The American Journey of West Point's Class of 1966*. New York: Henry Holt and Company, 1999.

Barkalow, Carol. *In the Men's House: An Inside Account of Life in the Army by One of West Point's First Female Graduates*. New York: Poseidon Press, 1990.

Blumenson, Martin *Patton: The Man Behind the Legend, 1885–1945*. New York: Morrow, 1985.

Bradley, Omar and Blair, Clay. *A General's Life: An Autobiography*. New York: Simon and Schuster, 1983.

Coffey, Thomas M. *Hap: The Story of the U.S. Air Force and the Man Who Built It, General Henry H. "Hap" Arnold*. New York: Viking Press, 1982.

Crackel, Theodore J. *The Illustrated History of West Point*. New York: Harry N. Abrams, 1991.

Davis, Benjamin O., Jr. *Benjamin O. Davis, Jr., American.* Washington, D.C.: Smithsonian Institution Press, 2000.

Ellis, Joseph and Moore, Robert. *School for Soldiers: West Point and the Profession of Arms.* New York: Oxford University Press, 1974.

Endler, James. *Other Leaders, Other Heroes: West Point's Legacy to America Beyond the Field of Battle.* Westport, Connecticut: Praeger Publishers, 1999.

Fleming, Thomas J. *West Point: The Men and Times of the United States Military Academy.* New York: William Morrow & Company, 1969.

Flipper, Henry O. *The Colored Cadet at West Point.* Lincoln, Nebraska: University of Nebraska Press, 1998.

Flipper, Henry O., and Harris, Theodore, ed. *Black Frontiersman: The Memoirs of Henry O. Flipper.* Fort Worth, Texas: Texas Christian University Press, 1997.

Forman, Sidney, ed. "Cadet Life before the Mexican War: Episodes in cadet life drawn from the manuscript collection in the Library of the United States Military Academy, excerpted from cadet letters." *USMA Library Bulletin No. 1,* USMA Printing Office, West Point, 1945.

Grant, Ulysses S. *Personal Memoirs of U. S. Grant.* New York: Charles L. Webster & Company, 1894.

James, D. Clayton. *The Years of MacArthur, Volume I 1880–1941.* Boston: Houghton Mifflin, 1970.

Leon, Philip W. *Bullies and Cowards: The West Point Hazing Scandal, 1898–1901.* Westport, Connecticut: Greenwood Press, 2000.

Lovell, John P. *Neither Athens Nor Sparta? The American Service Academies in Transition.* Bloomington, Indiana: Indiana University Press, 1979.

Morrison, James L., Jr. *"The Best School in the World": West Point, the Pre-Civil War Years, 1833–1866.* Kent, Ohio: Kent State University Press, 1986.

Pappas, George S. *To the Point: The United States Military Academy, 1802–1902.* Westport, Connecticut: Praeger Publishers, 1993.

Perret, Geoffrey. *Eisenhower.* New York: Random House, 1999.

————. *Old Soldiers Never Die: The Life of Douglas MacArthur.* Holbrook, Massachusetts: Adams Media Corporation, 1997.

Schaff, Morris. *The Spirit of Old West Point.* Boston: Houghton Mifflin Company, 1907.

Schwarzkopf, H. Norman. *It Doesn't Take a Hero: The Autobiography.* New York: Bantam Books, 1992.

Smith, Gene. *Lee and Grant.* New York: McGraw-Hill Book Company, 1984.

Stewart, Robert. *The Corps of Cadets: A Year at West Point.* Annapolis, Maryland: United States Naval Institute Press, 1996.

Utley, Robert M. *Cavalier in Buckskin: George Armstrong Custer and the Western Military Frontier* (Oklahoma Western Biographies, Vol. 1). Norman, Oklahoma: University of Oklahoma Press, 1991.

Waugh, John C. *The Class of 1846.* New York: Warner Books, 1994.

INDEX

Page numbers in red refer to illustrations.

John Grant is president and executive producer of Driftwood Productions, Inc. He created and executive produced the *West Point* television special seen on PBS. This is his fourth book. He wrote *Great American Rail Journeys* and coauthored, with Ray Jones, *Legendary Lighthouses* and *Legendary Lighthouses II*, the companion volumes to the PBS series. Grant has created, executive produced, and produced more than twenty-five hours of documentary programming for public television and cable. Prior to starting Driftwood Productions, Grant was the senior vice president of programming at PBS in Alexandria, Virginia. He lives with his wife, Joan, and son, Andy, in State College, Pennsylvania.

James M. Lynch has written and edited numerous books, educational videos, and CD-ROMs on a variety of topics for Time Life Books, the National Geographic Society, and other publishers. His most recent work was a history of the Ancient Olympic Games. This volume on West Point has allowed him to indulge his long-standing interest in the subject of military history. Lynch resides in Rhododendron, Oregon, with his wife, Maggie, his son, Mike, three cats, and two dogs.

Ronald H. Bailey has written sixteen books and contributed to more than a hundred others on subjects ranging from ancient history to modern warfare. His books include three on the American Civil War and four on World War II. He also is the author of a bicentennial history of Hartwick College. As a reporter at the *Cleveland Plain Dealer*, he specialized in military affairs. At the weekly *Life* magazine, where he was a correspondent, writer, and senior editor, his assignments included the Vietnam War, the U.S. Navy, and manned space flight. A native of Ohio, Bailey lives in rural upstate New York, where he and his wife, Sue, raised two sons and two daughters.

Experience

THE PAGEANTRY AND TRADITION OF THE HIT PBS™ SPECIAL